Also by Phillip C. McGraw, Ph.D.

Life Strategies

Life Strategies Workbook

Relationship Rescue

Relationship Rescue Workbook

Self Matters

THE SELF MATTERS COMPANION

Helping You Create Your Life
from the Inside Out

PHILLIP C. MCGRAW, PH.D.

THE FREE PRESS
New York London Toronto Sydney Singapore

*f*P

THE FREE PRESS
A Division of Simon & Schuster, Inc.
1230 Avenue of the Americas
New York, NY 10020

For information regarding special discounts for bulk purchases,
please contact Simon & Schuster Special Sales:
1-800-456-6798 or business@simonandschuster.com

Designed by Bonni Leon

Manufactured in the United States of America

10   9   8   7   6   5   4   3   2   3   1

Library of Congress Cataloging-in-Publication Data is available.

ISBN 0-7432-4296-3

To my wife,
Robin,
without whom I would not be living my best life;
and to my sons Jay and Jordan,
two amazing young men who humble me by being who they are;
and to my mother,
"Grandma Jerry,"
for making me feel special from day one,
and for showing me the true meaning of grace and courage
    under fire.

This book is also dedicated in memoriam to my father,
Joseph,
who never gave up and overcame tremendous odds to finally
    connect with his authentic self at the age of seventy-two.

ACKNOWLEDGMENTS

The writing of Self Matters *and* The Self Matters Companion *has been a wonderfully transformative yet sometimes difficult experience for me personally. It has been an undertaking that I could not have completed without the help and support of a number of important and in some instances "pivotal people" in my life.*

Thanks first to Robin, my wife and life partner of almost thirty years. Robin, you have been an inspirational and guiding force in my creating my own life from the inside out. It is your belief in and support of me that gave me the courage to step out and find my way back to my authentic self; back to being who I truly am instead of who others might want me to be. Without your spirit of adventure, I would to this very day be stuck in a life I did not want.

Thanks also to my boys, Jay and Jordan, for believing in and encouraging their dad. Both Jay and Jordan were at my side each day that I worked on this book. No messages of guilt, no long faces about the long hours, just support. That mattered greatly. Thanks, boys, for keeping me focused on what truly matters. In those times that I have found myself asking, "What's the point to all this scramble of life?" I have only to look at the hope and energy in your eyes and the answer is clear. I pray that as an adult I meet the standard of who you already are as young men.

I especially thank Oprah, my dear friend and a tremendously positive "pivotal person" in my life. It was a specific conversation with Oprah, riding along a desolate Texas road in the dead of winter, that inspired me to commit to one day demystifying the concept of self and creating a real world map for people to use in getting back to authenticity. Oprah, thanks for continuing to "raise the bar" for yourself and for me and for working to make a difference, and thanks for pulling me back into the work I love. Thanks, Oprah, for being in my balcony and allowing me to be in yours.

Thanks to Dr. Frank Lawlis for all of your input on content and writing as well. Frank was my major professor in graduate school, supervised my dissertation, and generally kept me on track. He helped when it would have been easier not to and has been a lifelong friend. We often debate whether he taught me everything I know or just everything he knows! Either way, he is in my opinion the leading authority in psychology today and his insight and analysis in this book was invaluable. As one of the few psychologists to ever hold diplomat status in both clinical and counseling psychology, he brought an expertise to this work that gave me great confidence that my views were on target.

Thanks to Deb Deford for the writing and organizational skills brought to bear on this book. Thanks, Deb, for the late nights and long weekends.

Thanks to Gary Dobbs, my partner, best friend, and godfather to my children, for your continuing support in everything I undertake in this life. You are invariably in my corner personally, professionally, and spiritually. Gary has long been on the shortest of "short lists" of "pivotal people" in my life and makes a huge difference each and every day.

Thanks to Jan Miller and all of her staff at Dupree Miller. Jan is *the* literary agent in the world today and has committed her energy and already unrivaled career to getting my message into the "hands of every person on the globe that can read"! (Jan never shoots low!) You are an amazing and tireless cheerleader whom it is impossible to be around without getting hugely "pumped"! Thanks, Jan, for being the consummate agent and gilt-edge professional that never gets tired, but, more important, thanks for being a great friend and supporter.

Thanks to Dave Khan, my publicist/PR guy/assistant/friend/tennis partner/never-say-no/make-it-happen guy. Dave lives and breathes our efforts to impact people's lives. Your gentle spirit and willingness to "take the plunge" so completely contributed mightily to creating the space, time, and energy essential to completing this project. Thanks, Dave, for running interference while I wrote like a hermit.

Thanks to Scott Madsen, who wakes up every morning saying "What can I do to help you do what you do?" Again, a friend and supporter who created the space, time, confidence, and energy that enabled me to be focused on this project.

I also thank Carolyn Reidy, president of Simon & Schuster, for passionately committing to the creation of this work.

Last but not least thanks to Dominick Anfuso, my in-house editor at the Free Press, for being so intimately involved with these books. Dominick, your input was invaluable and made these books much better. Thanks, Dominick, you are appreciated.

CONTENTS

INTRODUCTION

Millions of you have launched into the process of Self Matters, *creating your life from the inside out, and your e-mails and lectures have been both humbling and inspiring. Now, your learning about yourself and your relationship with yourself is about to go to the next level. You began an amazing process when you worked through your ten defining moments, your seven critical choices, and your five pivotal people. You continued that journey by looking at the internal factors that dictate and control your responses to those events. I'm back with more to say about you, who you have become and how you got there, and I'm doing it because you have asked me to do so.*

I refer to getting real about your authentic self as a process because it has a beginning but hopefully it has no end. This process is something that will become part of you managing you. *The Self Matters Companion* is designed to make this process part of your everyday life. It is designed to make this process something that becomes not just an exercise you once did but instead something that defines your commitment to living by design.

As the Life Law says, you either get it or you don't, and "getting it" means that you answer every question as completely and thoroughly as possible. That means that you have to add two very important patterns to your behavior. You must begin to consciously monitor yourself on a day-to-day basis, observing not only what you do but also how and why you do it. You must also constantly compare and contrast your actual real-world life with that which your authentic self desires and requires.

Having read so many of your letters, I also know that a fair number of you did not complete all of the assignments in *Self Matters*. (I'm sure you are the dutiful exception!) This is your chance to close any gaps in your understanding and build on what you already know.

I have said that the most important relationship you will ever have in this world is the one you have with yourself. In addition to this relationship being the most important one you'll ever have, I also want it to be the most successful one you will ever have. There is a very important formula for success in a relationship, and this formula applies whether the relationship you're managing is with yourself or with someone else. Here's the formula:

> The quality of a relationship is a function of the extent to which it is based on a solid underlying friendship and meets the needs of the two people involved.

As you embark on making the *Self Matters Companion* part of your daily life, think about how that formula can apply to you "companioning" you.

The first element of the formula, "based on a solid underlying friendship," is, I think, particularly intriguing when we are talking about what kind of friend you are to you.

Think about what characterizes your closest friendships with others. I'm betting that in those closest and most pleasing relationships, you, if you're a good friend, are accepting, devoted, loyal, fun-loving, honest, and genuine.

That is the goal and definition I hope you will carry forward in "companioning" yourself. This life has not and will not be a success-only journey. Not even close. If you bail on "you" when you observe less than desirable thoughts, feelings, or behaviors, you will be in big, big trouble. Do not be a fair-weather friend to yourself. Do not judge yourself when you stub your toe along the way. The *Self Matters Companion* will put you into intense and intimate contact with yourself day to day. Be loyal and stand by yourself!

The second element, "the extent to which it . . . meets the needs of the people involved," speaks to how effectively you are there for yourself. Throughout *Self Matters*, I wrote about identifying what you truly want and need to live consistently with your authentic self.

Hopefully, you can see how important that is to your relationship with yourself. You are a life manager, and you have one client and one client only: YOU! Do a good job because you can't fire yourself and get a replacement.

I can help you with what follows in these pages, but the doing is up to you. Be sure that you specifically, precisely identify your wants and needs and are deeply, loyally committed and you will have what you want. Bottom line, it's time to be there for you, not in thought or theory but in your walk through this everyday life.

1 WHAT IF . . . ?

Before you begin this portion of The Self Matters Companion *read chapter 1 (pages 1–26) of* Self Matters: Creating Your Life from the Inside Out.

I have a theory: I believe that many—maybe most—people in the hurry-up, make-do, look-good culture we're living in have settled way too cheap. A lot of us have given up our passion and let the colors fade out of our experience. We've settled for the appearance of an okay life instead of the substance of a *great* life. In the process, we've lost track of what is genuinely important to us. We've become couch potatoes in the parlor of life, overstimulated with input from the outside, and increasingly deaf to messages from the inside. We've gotten stuck in a ho-hum, "go along to get along" existence.

Now, you may be shaking your head and saying, "You've got it all wrong, Phil. My life *never* had the passion and color you're talking about." Maybe so. Or maybe you've let it slip away a tiny piece at a time—so slowly that you didn't even notice that it was happening. Either way, you've lost yourself in the rush of the world. But hear me on this. Your present and future don't have to continue in drab shades of gray.

Maybe you're shaking your head for another reason. Maybe you remember the days when your whole life seemed exciting and passionate. Maybe you invest more time and energy in reliving the old "glory days" than you do in creating new ones. That's just crazy. Life isn't a dress rehearsal and it isn't a rerun. If you are so busy daydreaming about the past that you settle for less than full, passionate, living color in the present, you're sleeping at the wheel and on your way to a wreck.

You may tell me, "I *like* my life. I'm doing fine." Hey, listen, I hope it's true. And if, after you hear me out and work your own way through this workbook, you still believe that, great! You'll know all the more confidently that you're making the most of the life and individuality you've been given. I'm betting that you're in for a surprise, and that you'll be thankful for it before you complete the last exercise in this workbook.

What I'm talking about is getting back to who you really are and what you really care about. I'm talking about learning to trust yourself, exercising the courage to be your real self, and making your life what you want it to be. I'm talking about claiming the right to live with excitement, passion, and confidence. Do yourself the most important favor you may ever have a chance at. Commit yourself to the few hours out of a lifetime it will take to read *Self Matters: Creating Your Life from the Inside Out* and complete the *Self Matters Companion*. Approach it with an open mind and a willing spirit. I'll be right here to guide you. Let's go!

AH, THE GOOD OL' DAYS

It's no good to spend all your time reliving the "good ol' days." But there's a lot to learn if you can let your memories take you back to a truer you. Read each of the phrases below and finish each thought with at least fifty words about yourself. Don't worry about grammar or spelling. That stuff doesn't matter here. This is for you and you alone. Be specific and concrete. Include time, place, circumstances, who you were with, what was happening, what you were doing, and any other details you can remember. Pay special attention to how you felt.

1. I remember a particular time when I was especially happy, and it was

2. Sometimes, I felt really excited, but one time that stands out is when

3. I remember times when a person said something to me or treated me in such a way that it made a positive difference in my life, and one of those times was when

4. A time when I felt really special to someone was when I

5. When I was younger, I always wanted to

6. What I desire most deeply is to

7. If I could be or do anything I wanted to do, I would

8. I used to dream about myself as

9. If I could learn anything, I would choose to learn

10. What interests me most is (*name at least five interests*)

11. When I fantasize about myself, I am

12. I wish people would see me as

13. Before my life is over I want to

14. If I could, I would dedicate my life to

15. My secret desire always has been to

AUTHENTICITY LITMUS TEST

Let's take a closer look at how you're living right now. If you want to make the changes that will help you live authentically now and in the future, you need to know where you are. Have you been passively accepting what life throws at you and ignoring who you really are? Have you even been choosing behaviors that keep you from an authentic life? Or are your choices and circumstances flowing from your authentic self? The following exercise is designed to help you see how you're doing. Read each of the statements below and circle the number under the response that best reflects how you're living right now. Be as honest as you can. Anything less is a waste of your time and effort.

	Never	Sometimes	Often	Always
I am constantly tired, stressed, emotionally flat, or even depressed, worried, and unhappy.	1	2	3	4
My life includes things I profess to hate, but I continue to do them anyway.	1	2	3	4
My life is dominated by anxiety and worry, but I'm not doing anything to change it.	1	2	3	4
My mind has gotten dull and I don't give much time to new ideas or possibilities.	1	2	3	4
My emotions are marked by cynicism, apathy, hopelessness, and a lack of optimism.	1	2	3	4
I am choosing and behaving in ways that are based on what I think others expect or want.	1	2	3	4

Scoring

6–10   You've stayed in touch with the real you and, for the most part, make choices that reflect who you are and what you care about. Consider this an opportunity to continue to learn about yourself and keep growing, to "polish up" the positive momentum of your life.

11–15   You may have some sense of who you are and what you care about, but you are making compromises that put your authentic self at risk. It's time to stop moving in the direction you're going and make the changes that will help you be who you really want to be.

16–20   You may be on the right road, but you're driving in the wrong direction. This is the perfect moment to make a U-turn and start getting rid of the lies and misperceptions that are distorting your view of you and your life.

21–24   It's time for you to get real. You're cheating yourself and the people you love of a lot of happiness and fulfillment, because you're making choices that are eroding the quality of your life. I know you care about the quality of your life, and *right now* is

the time to commit to significant changes that help you redis-
cover the strong, loving, worthy individual you are.

WHAT DO YOU WANT?

What sorts of changes will begin to shape a life that fits the real you?
What elements are missing from your life right now that would help to
bring your world in line with the person that you truly, authentically
are? What do you want? What do you need to be part of your life?
Using the list below, put a checkmark to the left of any item that you'd
like to make a part—or a bigger part—of your life. Add any additional
items that are important to you, using the blank lines at the end of the
list. Now look at each of the items you've checked. I want you to think
seriously about each and then indicate *how important they actually are
to you,* using one of the symbols defined below.

* = I would give my life for this.

o = I would sacrifice a lot, but not all, for this.

= I want this enough to go to some trouble for it.

• = I wouldn't do much to have this.

√ here		importance
	Music	
	Art	
	Work	
	Kids	
	Spiritual life	
	Honesty	
	Free time	
	Pride in work	
	Pride in appearance	
	Living with dignity	
	Health	
	Being in nature	
	A career that uses my strengths	
	Permission to say, do, and be who I am	
	Volunteer work	

√ here		importance
	Hobby	
	Different lifestyle	
	Passion	
	Excitement	
	Independence	
	Meaningful relationship	
	Different body condition	
	Feeling like a giver	
	Extended family	
	Community where I live	

Look back over what you've checked and the importance you've indicated that it has for you. What's keeping you from pursuing those items you've checked *and* starred? Do you know? What would it take to make them more a part of your life? Keep these questions in mind as you continue to work through this book. You're on the road to a more authentic, reality-based life that can unlock your true passion, strengths, gifts, and talents. But first you have to confront the ways in which you've cheated yourself with deluded thinking and distorted perceptions. That's the adventure ahead. You're on your way. Keep going!

JOURNAL EXERCISE

There's an old saying that goes like this: "If you aim for nothing, you're sure to reach it." The fact that you've taken on this workbook proves that you're aiming for a whole lot more than nothing. Let's see if we can get a more specific picture of where you want to be in the future. Read each of the following phrases, then complete the thought with at least a paragraph. If you need more space use extra paper, but be sure that you keep the paper with your workbook. You'll want to refer to what you've written later on. This is an excellent chance to get in touch with some of the things you've been missing.

Remember: this and everything else you write in this workbook is TOTALLY CONFIDENTIAL AND FOR YOUR EYES ONLY. Don't worry about whether you're a "good" writer or how well you spell. It doesn't matter at all. The important thing is that you dig deep and get honest with yourself. Write from the heart, and keep writing until you've said everything on the subject that you can. Please don't skip this step. It's a crucial part of what you're going to do to make your life much, much better. Not only that, it's fun! So get going.

1. One of the things I hope to find out about myself is . . .

2. I need to know why I . . .

3. In my relationship, I want (don't want) to share . . .

4. This time next year, I'd like my job to be . . .

5. By the time I finish this workbook, I would like to be able to . . .

SUM IT UP
Take a minute to put in writing what you've rediscovered about your-self in the preceding exercises. In a short paragraph, describe the "you" that is beginning to emerge.

2 DEFINING THE AUTHENTIC SELF

Before you begin this portion of The Self Matters Companion, *read chapter 2 (pages 27–64) of* Self Matters: Creating Your Life from the Inside Out.

So much for the warm-up. You're about to discover that you have a lot more choice in your life than you can even imagine. You'll learn how to look honestly at your life and unravel how you got to where you are right now. You'll discover that you can refuse to accept the life you're living if it doesn't truly reflect who you are. But before you can travel farther along this road, you need to have a clearer grasp of the answer to a very short, but not at all simple, question: "Who are you?"

Keep in mind that, more often than not, when a person seems to answer this question, he or she is actually sidestepping it. The person may tell you what he or she does for a living, what role he or she fills in the lives of others, or some qualitative judgment about self that he or she has been fed by the world. But you never get a real answer to the actual question. In fact, you may be just such a person: you can't answer the question, "Who are you?" because you honestly don't know the answer.

I want to assure you again that there *is* an authentic self inside you. There are no exceptions to this, including you. The authentic you may be buried under a pile of other people's expectation, but that core self exists and is accessible to you if you're willing to do the work to reconnect to your strengths and values in a meaningful way. You have a unique set of gifts, skills, abilities, interests, talents, insights, and wisdom. They came to you free of charge—a gift of your creation—and when they are allowed full expression, they give you your happiest, most satisfying, and rewarding moments in life.

It takes an enormous amount of energy to be what you are not. Yet this is exactly what happens when you suppress your authentic self and let your fictional self—that being built on the judgments, demands, and expectations of others—rule. On the other hand, as you learn more and more how to throw off your fictional self and unleash your authentic self, you'll feel a terrific energy lifting and carrying you forward. You'll feel inspired and healed.

The exercises in this chapter are designed to help you deal with hard, objective fact instead of opinions and assumptions. I want you to challenge every single thing you have ever believed about yourself, to be skeptical of familiar patterns and information. Listen more deeply to yourself. Don't fall back on the easy answers. Let your gut speak. Everything you write here is for you alone. You can let your true self speak out here without fear of anyone else's judgment.

THE BEST ME

In some native cultures, young people undergo a "coming-of-age" ritual. While the ritual often has aspects intended to bind the young person to his or her community, it often also is meant to help a young person identify his or her unique strengths and qualities. Whether the ritual includes choosing a name, discovering a song, or communicating the unique vibration of one's soul, it allows the individual to connect with and express what is at the heart of who he or she is.

Find a quiet place where you won't be interrupted or distracted and, right now, give your best attention to tuning in to your innermost self. Find words that seem to you to describe yourself in each of the following ways. You don't need to write sentences unless it helps you find ways to express what you mean. It's only important that you quiet the negative voices and assessments that you usually carry around with you and instead focus on the many positive qualities that make you unique.

Intellectually, I am . . .

Spiritually, I am . . .

Physically, I am . . .

Emotionally, I am . . .

MY HERO!

If it's true that there's more to you than you've been living, you probably didn't find it an easy task to identify some of your best and deepest qualities. Yet until you can get past your fictional self to the authentic you, you'll remain imprisoned, unable to be all that you can be for yourself, your family, and the world. Another, less direct way to uncover the qualities that you value most is to consider the people you hold in highest regard. They may be people in your family or community, a mentor or pastor, someone in the news, or someone whose name lives on in history.

The question is: "Who are your heroes?" The people you admire the most tell a lot about you. Right now, list five people you consider "heroes" in your own life or in the world, today or in the past. Don't cheat on this. Choose people whom *you* really believe to be heroes, not the people you would expect others to choose or whom you think you *ought* to respect and admire. If you're really going to recover your authentic self, you need to practice every ounce of courage and honesty you can.

1. _____
2. _____
3. _____
4. _____
5. _____

Which one of the people you just listed would you put at the *top* of your "hero" list? Use the space below to describe *why* that person is top-of-the-list for you. Include every quality and/or behavior that makes that person unique and special—that is, worthy of "hero" status.

AUTHENTICITY SCALE

As you've thought about your own best qualities and the characteristics you admire in a hero, you've probably begun to see some of the ways in which you've let the best of you disappear. I'm going to guide you on a journey back to you. But first I want you to get a greater sense of how much of your life energy you are giving to your authentic self and how much you are using up on a fictional self.

Each numbered item below includes two statements. You can think of these as the "polar alternatives." You may find that the description on the left describes you best, or you may find that the one on the right does. What you need to do is consider which of the alternatives best describes *you*. I've given you a choice of four different ways to rate yourself on that spectrum. For each item, read both choices, then put an "X" under the one that best describes you.

The Fictional Self	True All of the Time of the Left (1)	True Most of the Time of the Left (2)	True Most of the Time of the Right (3)	True All of the Time of the Right (4)	The Authentic Self
1. I am motivated by a need to please authority and win approval from others.	( )	( )	( )	( )	I am motivated by internal factors, such as a sense of a mission in life and honest thinking about myself.
2. I follow orders for fear of disapproval.	( )	( )	( )	( )	I make choices based on best self-interest.
3. I lack confidence to function without authority figures; I lack initiative.	( )	( )	( )	( )	I am confident to function effectively with self-decisions.
4. My self-esteem is based on what others think; I desperately want approval.	( )	( )	( )	( )	My self-esteem is defined internally with or without external approval.
5. I have difficulty in seeing connection between personal behavior and consequences without others' reactions.	( )	( )	( )	( )	I am able to see connection between personal behavior and consequences.

The Fictional Self	True All of the Time of the Left (1)	True Most of the Time of the Left (2)	True Most of the Time of the Right (3)	True All of the Time of the Right (4)	The Authentic Self
6. I have difficulty making choices based on personal priorities.	( )	( )	( )	( )	I am able to make choices based on self-priorities.
7. I have feelings of dependency and fear.	( )	( )	( )	( )	I have feelings of self-confidence and strength.
8. I avoid internal feelings.	( )	( )	( )	( )	I seek internal knowledge.
9. I am compliant to others.	( )	( )	( )	( )	I am cooperative with others.
10. I am oriented to avoid punishment.	( )	( )	( )	( )	I am oriented to self-fulfillment.
11. I am generally uneasy about what people expect of me.	( )	( )	( )	( )	I am usually confident around other people.
12. I feel frightened most of the time.	( )	( )	( )	( )	I am happy with myself most of the time.
13. I feel lost in my life.	( )	( )	( )	( )	I have a purpose to my life.
14. I always feel as if I do not belong here.	( )	( )	( )	( )	I have a kinship with everyone.
15. I hate to make decisions.	( )	( )	( )	( )	I enjoy making decisions.
16. I hate myself most of the time.	( )	( )	( )	( )	I am amazed at myself.
17. I cannot forgive myself.	( )	( )	( )	( )	I have made mistakes, but I have learned from them.
18. I call myself names like "stupid" and "dummy."	( )	( )	( )	( )	I appraise myself honestly and objectively.
19. I feel like a loser.	( )	( )	( )	( )	I am a winner.

The Fictional Self	True All of the Time of the Left (1)	True Most of the Time of the Left (2)	True Most of the Time of the Right (3)	True All of the Time of the Right (4)	The Authentic Self
20. I still hear my parents talk to me in my head.	( )	( )	( )	( )	I have let go of my parents' judgments.
21. I worry that I am going to screw up.	( )	( )	( )	( )	I cannot let pessimism into my life.
22. I always wonder if others are evaluating me.	( )	( )	( )	( )	I pay attention to my values rather than others'.
23. I often wonder why despite my best efforts it seems so hard to get what you want in life.	( )	( )	( )	( )	I find it simple to obtain what I want in life because I can focus correctly.
24. When I am alone I find myself staring into space and feeling disconnection.	( )	( )	( )	( )	When I am alone I find I am good company and I enjoy my space.
25. When I cannot sleep I wonder how I am going to make it through the next day.	( )	( )	( )	( )	When I cannot sleep I allow my mind to be creative, knowing that tomorrow will be exciting and rewarding.
26. I find that hope and joy give way to tired "going through the motions of life" feelings.	( )	( )	( )	( )	I find hope and joy easy to experience.
27. I often find it hard to get off my butt and get into the game.	( )	( )	( )	( )	I find it easy to get started on a new project.
28. I often worry why other people are successful and I am not.	( )	( )	( )	( )	I find it easy to understand why other people are successful.
29. I am usually in the grips of depression and anxiety.	( )	( )	( )	( )	I am usually happy and hopeful.

The Fictional Self	True All of the Time of the Left (1)	True Most of the Time of the Left (2)	True Most of the Time of the Right (3)	True All of the Time of the Right (4)	The Authentic Self
30. I am often frustrated and want to just give up and scream.	( )	( )	( )	( )	I can handle frustrations.
31. I often wonder why I am never the boss or respected as a leader.	( )	( )	( )	( )	I am often the boss and respected.
32. I struggle to comprehend why my marriage is hard and my children are not adjusting well.	( )	( )	( )	( )	My family life is secure and comforting.
33. I want to run away from the world, especially when the bills come.	( )	( )	( )	( )	I find life fun and bills just a small part of life.
34. I feel that I am living a masquerade life, not one of my own.	( )	( )	( )	( )	I am living my own life.
35. I am sick and tired of my life.	( )	( )	( )	( )	My life is wonderful and exciting.
36. I shake my head when I commit to starting a new job, a new diet, etc., because I will probably fail.	( )	( )	( )	( )	I look forward to new challenges, knowing that success is possible.
37. I have come to the conclusion that I am living a life that I did not design or want.	( )	( )	( )	( )	I am living my life, my purpose.
38. I am bitter about my life and how it has turned out.	( )	( )	( )	( )	I am not bitter but I am glad I designed my life, however it has worked out.

Scoring

For every X in column 1, give yourself a 1   _____

For every X in column 2, give yourself a 2   _____

For every X in column 3, give yourself a 3   _____

For every X in column 4, give yourself a 4   _____

Total your points here: _____

Find the range in which your score falls. The description for your score will give you a first look at how much of your life energy you are giving to your authentic self and how much you are using up on a fictional self.

38–70   This range suggests that you are seriously disconnected from your authentic self. Ask yourself how much of your experience of life is what you really want.

71–110   This range suggests that most of the time you are operating from a distorted fictional self-concept rather than from who you really are. You may be often confused about what you should be doing or how best to use your time. You may be bewildered about what the world expects of you. In this range, you may be aware of your fictional self and know that you could change your life, but you may also fear the responsibility of change.

111–129   This score indicates that your self-concept is distorted into a fictional version at least some of the time. While you may be afraid to be totally yourself because of the world's power over you, you may also want desperately to serve your authenticity. The problem is, in this range, a person often lets himself or herself down when challenges get too great.

130–142   In this range, you are fortunate enough to operate mostly in tune with your authenticity. You have a clear idea of your authentic self and what you want from life. When faced with difficulties, you look naturally into the self so that goals remain clear and consistent with your authenticity.

TEST OF CONGRUENCY

The profile that follows will help you see the degree to which your current life experience—how you are thinking, feeling, and living—compares to what your experience would be if you were living an ideal, fully authentic, and fulfilling life. This test takes you through a three-step process.

First, you will describe your full potential by rating yourself on certain dimensions *as you would be at your best.*

Second, you'll rate yourself on the same dimensions, this time as those dimensions reflect *who and what you believe you really are.*

Third, you will determine the percentage of difference between the two. The comparison will give you an early benchmark as to the health of your self-concept and the extent to which you are living true to yourself.

Step 1: Circle all the words that you think describe the ideal person you want to be, the person you believe is the full potential of who you are and will ever be.

pretty   attractive   beautiful   cute   nice-looking   appealing   cool   sweet spiritual   wise   nice   friendly   faithful   leader   strong   supportive   moral ethical   principled   good   honest   decent   warm   loving   tender warmhearted   demonstrative   caring   kind   affectionate   cordial   hospitable welcoming   amiable   cheerful   passionate   fiery   enthusiastic   zealous arrogant   egocentric   altruistic   sympathetic   humane   selfless   philanthropic smart   dependent   free   gentle   thoughtful   domineering   submissive autonomous   creative   compassionate   self-sufficient   private   liberated conventional   objective   elegant   clever   stylish   intelligent   quick   charming tidy   neat   thoughtful   attentive   careful   watchful   alert   reliable   inspired inventive   resourceful   ingenious   productive   exciting   energetic   lively vigorous   bouncy   active   joyful   blissful   pleased   ecstatic   cheery   sane rational   sensible   reasonable   normal   complete   capable   genuine inspiring   proud   approachable   peaceful   honest   giving   nurturing accomplished whole perfect undivided achiever great confident compassionate content humble unassuming happy satisfied comfortable at ease relaxed able knowledgeable skilled proficient expert adept rich wealthy affluent prosperous full gorgeous valuable abundant fruitful powerful deep prolific understanding dynamic useful helpful constructive beneficial positive functional worthwhile

Now count the number of words you circled in Step 1. This will be called the Total Potential Score. Your Total Potential Score is_____.

Step 2: Now circle the words below that describe how you *actually are* at present.

pretty attractive beautiful cute nice-looking appealing cool sweet spiritual wise nice friendly faithful leader strong supportive moral ethical principled good honest decent warm loving tender warmhearted demonstrative caring kind affectionate cordial hospitable welcoming amiable cheerful passionate fiery enthusiastic zealous arrogant egocentric altruistic sympathetic humane selfless philanthropic smart dependent free gentle thoughtful domineering submissive autonomous creative compassionate self-sufficient private liberated conventional objective elegant clever stylish intelligent quick charming tidy neat thoughtful attentive careful watchful alert reliable inspired inventive resourceful ingenious productive exciting energetic lively vigorous bouncy active joyful blissful pleased ecstatic cheery sane rational sensible reasonable normal complete capable genuine inspiring proud approachable peaceful honest giving nurturing accomplished whole perfect undivided achiever great confident compassionate content humble unassuming happy satisfied comfortable at ease relaxed able knowledgeable skilled proficient expert adept rich wealthy affluent prosperous full gorgeous valuable abundant fruitful powerful deep prolific understanding dynamic useful helpful constructive beneficial positive functional worthwhile

Now count the number of words you circled in Step 2. This will be called the Actual Self Score. Your Actual Self Score is _____.

Step 3: The Congruency Score is the percentage of words you circled in Step 2 (Actual Self Score) as compared to the total words scored in Step 1 (Total Potential Score).

$$\text{Congruency Score} = \frac{\text{Actual Self Score}}{\text{Total Potential Score}} \times 100 = \underline{\qquad}\%$$

If you are uncomfortable figuring out your score mathematically, you can use the table here to get an estimate, which you can fill in above.

Actual Self Score				
81–90	60%	64%	69%	75%
71–80	53%	57%	62%	67%
61–70	47%	50%	54%	58%
51–60	40%	43%	46%	50%
41–50	33%	36%	38%	42%
31–40	27%	29%	30%	33%
21–30	20%	22%	23%	25%
11–20	13%	14%	15%	17%
0–10	7%	7%	8%	8%
	141–150	131-140	121–130	111–120

Congruency Score

Total Potential Score

SCORING

If your score is 90 to 100 percent: You are operating in your **full potential** range most of the time, finding happiness and joy from within. You are fulfilling your mission as you see it and probably have good mental health.

If your score is 75 to 89 percent: You are in the positive range of **living consistently with your authentic self.** You have escaped serious damage to your personal truth. You have good self-esteem that will help you be successful.

If your score is 50 to 74 percent: You are in the positive range and have realized **some good aspects** of who you are. However, you are missing some important aspects, powerful strengths, and goals that are true to your authentic self. You very likely have some self-doubt and lack of self-confidence in truly appreciating your potential.

If your score is 35 to 49 percent: You are limiting yourself and using only a small part of who you really are, because you have listened to the world telling you who you are instead of being guided by an undistorted personal truth and self-concept. Much work is needed.

If your score is 1 to 34 percent: You are living in your fictional self. Your personal truth and self-concept have been seriously damaged and distorted. You are wasting precious life energy. Your power is infected with fictional concepts and your efforts are misdirected to goals that are not your own.

WHAT'S HOLDING YOU BACK?

Are you beginning to see how the world has distracted you from your unique, individual potential and core self? The good news is that now that you are becoming aware of all that you can be, you can continue on the journey toward authenticity with more power and motivation. In fact, you may be wondering why you didn't do so a long time ago. I'll give you a one-word answer that almost certainly lies at the heart of why you got off track in the first place and have continued there: fear. Fear of change is common currency among human beings. And not only are *you* fearful of changing, *others* have all sorts of fears about you changing. The ruts we get into, no matter how damaging or limiting, are at least familiar and predictable. Stepping up and out of those ruts is scary.

So let's face the bogeyman and get him out into the light of day. Assume that you will have fear. Let's take it apart. What fears have kept you from changing in the past? What kind of fear do you expect to feel when you change? In the spaces provided below, respond to these two questions as they relate to the key word I've provided. Remember that this exercise is for your eyes only. Be as specific and honest as you know how to be.

Family

God

Children

Spouse

Friends

Your Job

Look through what you've just written. What common themes do you see? Fear of losing? Not being loved or respected? Fear of failure or of aging? The fears that you are bringing out into the open here do not have to continue to hold you back. In fact, I'm telling you that you will be immersed in a series of challenges as you work through this book, and they will demand a commitment of heart and soul. Make that commitment right now. Trust me; you will never regret it.

THINK ABOUT IT

You've just taken another big step toward understanding where you are and where you could be. Take a moment right now to look back over the questions in this section and the answers you gave to them. After you've done this, consider what new insights you have gained in the process. In the space below, write a paragraph about what you've discovered.

3 YOUR SELF-CONCEPT

Before you begin this portion of The Self Matters Companion, *read chapter 3 (pages 65–87) of* Self Matters: Creating Your Life from the Inside Out.

You, like everyone, have an idea of yourself—a "self-concept"—that includes an array of beliefs, facts, opinions, and perceptions. You carry this idea of yourself into every moment of every day of your life. The problem is, there is much in this self-concept that is not even known to you. Yet it exerts a powerful influence on you and how you present yourself to the world. In many ways, it determines your life, because it is the root of all that you do and feel and *how* you do and feel it.

Another way of saying this is that your concept of yourself, regardless of how aware you are of it, determines the manner in which you engage with others (and even yourself) in your life. In turn, that draws the kind of response you get from them.

Remember: your self-concept has a history. It has developed over a lifetime as you have accumulated experiences, both positive and negative, internal and external. You cannot change your life for the better unless and until you change your concept of yourself to reflect your authentic self. And you can't begin to *redefine* your self-concept until you've discovered what it actually is right now.

The coming chapters are designed to help you unpack your past so that you can walk out of it into the present and future with new passion and power. They'll help you dig deep into the internal and external factors that have formed your self-concept up until today. For now, I want to start the demystifying process with a few simple, helpful exercises. Give focused time to completing these exercises. That means sending the kids out to play, turning off the television, scheduling a date with yourself, or whatever else is needed for you to put aside distractions. As you put into writing your own responses to a number of guiding thoughts and input from others, I guarantee that you will begin to uncover thoughts and opinions about yourself that you never knew you had. Only as you bring these concepts to the surface and face them squarely will you be able to gauge their accuracy and either nurture or eradicate them.

This is the absolutely essential first step toward finding your core, authentic self and living consistently with it. The investment you make will determine how productive this step is. It is a foundation for what is to come. Give it your best. You're worth it!

I AM . . .

Let's begin with a bit of guided reflection. As always, don't worry about spelling or grammar. This is not a test and no one is going to grade you on your ability to write. Just record the thoughts that come to your mind as they come.

I've given you a series of phrases below. Please finish each of the statements about yourself. Expand your responses to be at least fifty words in length.

I am very good when . . .

I think of myself as being . . .

I think my body is . . .

I am happiest when . . .

My greatest strengths are . . .

I am best in situations that . . .

I think I could be . . .

I fear . . .

What keeps me from being what I really want is . . .

In the future, I . . .

What keeps me going is . . .

No one knows that I . . .

If I described myself as a plant, such as a tree or flower, I would be . . .

If I described myself as a car, I would be . . .

If I described myself as an animal, I would be . . .

You may have found this exercise fun, or you may have found it challenging. Maybe you got a charge out of thinking of your strengths or imagining your future. Maybe you don't usually spend a lot of time thinking of yourself as a car. That's all okay. Each of the phrases above gives you an opportunity to tune in to more of your self-concept. Before you move on, read over what you've written. Are there any questions for which you wrote something other than your first real response? Was there any item for which you said, "Well, I'm not going to write *that!*"? Was there any phrase that you didn't really want to answer? Right now, I want you to go back and write what you chose *not* to write the first time through. You don't have to erase anything, just add the new stuff on. Those thoughts that you edited out before you could write them are just as important as the thoughts you chose to record. What you write is for your eyes only, and you should be sure to keep your workbook in a place that is safe. I can't emphasize enough how important it is that you be as honest and complete in your answers as possible. Once you've given your best to this exercise, you're ready to move on.

WHO DO YOU THINK THAT I AM?

This is a fascinating and enlightening exercise that takes a little courage and some effort, but offers enormous rewards in terms of learning how you appear to the world. Select five people whom you know and who have some knowledge of you. These should be people you trust as individuals. You may select a friend, your spouse, your children, your parent, a person at work, another family member, or even a former teacher. What you are going to do is conduct a brief interview with *you* as the subject of conversation.

This does not have to be face-to-face. It can be done on the telephone or even on the Internet. The goal is to gather feedback in a non-defensive way about how you come across to others. You'll be asking people to lend you a little assistance that takes very little time and no preparation on their side. Most people are more than willing to participate, if asked. A few ground rules for you to observe:

- **Try to record as much as you can from this experience,** if you conduct your interview orally. You may think you'll remember what is said and how it is said, but you won't. Memory is a slippery thing, especially if you feel embarrassed or flustered.
- **Please do not try to argue with the person,** especially if the individual says something good, but also in the case of some negative elements. You can believe or not believe it. Just listen and consider the information.
- **Commit yourself to taking responsibility for the information you gather.** There's nothing worse than asking someone for an opinion and then holding it against them in some way. If you're going to do this interview and benefit from it, you have to play fair.

Here is a possible script for you to use:

"I am doing a 'Dr. Phil' course (from the *Oprah* show) on how to be more successful in my life, and I would like you to give me a little honest feedback about how I have come across at times. I want to ask you about ten questions. These are all phrased in a positive way because I need to know my strengths, not my weaknesses. I want you to tell me what you think and then give me a concrete example, if you can think of one. I don't want to make you feel uncomfortable, but this would be important and helpful for me to know."

Person #1: _____ (*name*)

1. Please describe something that I consistently do well.
   Interviewee:

   You:

2. Please name one thing you have seen me do well.
   Interviewee:

   You:

3. Please tell me the best thing about how I look.
   Interviewee:

   You:

4. In as much detail as possible, can you remember any time that I seemed to be happiest?
   Interviewee:

   You:

5. Tell me what you think my strongest traits are.
   Interviewee:

   You:

6. If you were going to describe my best strengths with three words, what would they be?
   Interviewee:

   You:

7. If you were in a situation in which you thought I could help you in some way, what would that situation be?
   Interviewee:

   You:

8. Can you tell me any aspect you respect about me?
   Interviewee:

   You:

9. If you had to describe me as a car, what kind of car would I be? Why?
   Interviewee:

   You:

10. If you had to describe me as an animal, what kind of animal would I be? Why?
    Interviewee:

    You:

When the interview is over, thank the person who agreed to help you and postpone any further conversation until later. Then sit down alone with your interview and, alongside of each of the interviewees statement about you, express how you feel about what was said. Continue with the remaining four interviews, using the forms provided here.

Person #2: _____ (*name*)

1. Please describe something that I consistently do well.
   Interviewee:

   You:

2. Please name one thing you have seen me do well.
   Interviewee:

You:

3. Please tell me the best thing about how I look.
   Interviewee:

   You:

4. In as much detail as possible, can you remember any time that I seemed to be happiest?
   Interviewee:

   You:

5. Tell me what you think my strongest traits are.
   Interviewee:

   You:

6. If you were going to describe my best strengths with three words, what would they be?
   Interviewee:

   You:

7. If you were in a situation in which you thought I could help you in some way, what would that situation be?
    Interviewee:

    You:

8. Can you tell me any aspect you respect about me?
    Interviewee:

    You:

9. If you had to describe me as a car, what kind of car would I be? Why?
    Interviewee:

    You:

10. If you had to describe me as an animal, what kind of animal would I be? Why?
    Interviewee:

    You:

Person #3: _____ *(name)*

1. Please describe something that I consistently do well.
   Interviewee:

   You:

2. Please name one thing you have seen me do well.
   Interviewee:

   You:

3. Please tell me the best thing about how I look.
   Interviewee:

   You:

4. In as much detail as possible, can you remember any time that I seemed to be happiest?
   Interviewee:

   You:

5. Tell me what you think my strongest traits are.
    Interviewee:

    You:

6. If you were going to describe my best strengths with three words, what would they be?
    Interviewee:

    You:

7. If you were in a situation in which you thought I could help you in some way, what would that situation be?
    Interviewee:

    You:

8. Can you tell me any aspect you respect about me?
    Interviewee:

    You:

9. If you had to describe me as car what kind of car would I be? Why?
   Interviewee:

   You:

10. If you had to describe me as an animal, what kind of animal would I be? Why?
    Interviewee:

    You:

Person #4: _____ *(name)*

1. Please describe something that I consistently do well.
   Interviewee:

   You:

2. Please name one thing you have seen me do well.
   Interviewee:

   You:

3. Please tell me the best thing about how I look.
   Interviewee:

You:

4. In as much detail as possible, can you remember any time that I seemed to be happiest?
   Interviewee:

   You:

5. Tell me what you think my strongest traits are.
   Interviewee:

   You:

6. If you were going to describe my best strengths with three words, what would they be?
   Interviewee:

   You:

7. If you were in a situation in which you thought I could help you in some way, what would that situation be?
   Interviewee:

   You:

8. Can you tell me any aspect you respect about me?
Interviewee:

You:

9. If you had to describe me as a car, what kind of car would I be? Why?
Interviewee:

You:

10. If you had to describe me as an animal, what kind of animal would I be? Why?
Interviewee:

You:

Person #5: _____ *(name)*

1. Please describe something that I consistently do well.
Interviewee:

You:

2. Please name one thing you have seen me do well.
   Interviewee:

   You:

3. Please tell me the best thing about how I look.
   Interviewee:

   You:

4. In as much detail as possible, can you remember any time that I seemed to be happiest?
   Interviewee:

   You:

5. Tell me what you think my strongest traits are.
   Interviewee:

   You:

6. If you were going to describe my best strengths with three words, what would they be?
   Interviewee:

You:

7. If you were in a situation in which you thought I could help you in some way, what would that situation be?
   Interviewee:

   You:

8. Can you tell me any aspect you respect about me?
   Interviewee:

   You:

9. If you had to describe me as a car, what kind of car would I be? Why?
   Interviewee:

   You:

10. If you had to describe me as an animal, what kind of animal would I be? Why?
    Interviewee:

    You:

SELF-CONCEPT INVENTORY

If you've completed the exercises in this chapter so far, you've made some headway in tuning in to your self-concept. What I want you to do now is pull together the ground you've covered. In the space provided below, write a one-paragraph response to each of the questions. Draw on both your own responses and the responses you received in the interviews.

What have you learned about yourself through this process?

What took you by surprise?

How has this process changed how you feel about you?

4 YOUR TEN DEFINING MOMENTS

Before you begin this portion of The Self Matters Companion, *read the "Introduction to External Factors" section (pages 88–97) and chapter 4 (pages 98–123) of* Self Matters: Creating Your Life from the Inside Out.

By now, you are beginning to recognize that your self-concept, life choices, and outcomes have their roots in your personal history. A general understanding of an abstract idea, however, isn't going to change your life. For a genuine life change, you need to get real *about you.* You need to do the hard work of digging into the real facts of your own experiences and uncover the events and people who have contributed to making you who you are and how you are today.

The exercises that follow are designed to help you unearth ten of the most influential events of your life, which I have called your "Defining Moments." Keep in mind that these events may very well be of little interest or import to anyone who did not live them from inside your skin. It's absolutely essential, however, that you remember this truth: If it's important to *you*, it's important.

The chart shown here is meant to help trigger some memories; it is by no means a complete list. Your defining moments are the outlines of your life and may, in fact, fit into rather different categories. Regardless, you need to be aware of them, and for the following exercise to be useful, you need to require of yourself the most detailed and thorough memory you can muster. Find a quiet spot, commit real time, and have extra paper on hand in case you need more writing space. Write to yourself, knowing that what you recall is *totally confidential and for your eyes only*. Now review the chart, then follow the directions for each step of the exercise.

Age Groups	Characteristic Defining Moments and Memories
1 to 5 years old	• interactions with family • playing games • going to nursery school for the first time • learning to sleep in the dark • noticing people aging
6 to 12 years old	• grade-school years • teacher replacing parent for the first time • sibling types to cope with • having to prove yourself in a new group
13 to 20 years old	• turmoil and frustration • learning about being an adult • breaking away from the family • discovering the "big deal" about sex • social relations taking on primary importance • whether you belong to the "in" crowd • love • rites of passage or initiations • thinking about the future
21 to 38 years old	• beginning life as a citizen of the community • jobs • responsibility for a family • learning how to be a partner in life • learning how to be a parent

- dealing with lack of knowledge, power, or self-discipline
- newfound admiration for our parents or other role models

39 to 55 years old
- beginning a new era of life
- settling into vocation and future expectations
- stable living situation
- paying more attention to yourself

56 years old and beyond
- thoughts of retirement from work
- release from some family and community responsibilities
- losing some physical vitality
- confronting more limitations
- turning over responsibilities to others
- getting to know others in more intimate, less competitive ways

YOUR TEN DEFINING MOMENTS

Only you will know when and in what circumstances the defining moments of your life occurred. Take time to think through the various stages of the life you have lived so far. You may want to deal with only one age range in a single sitting. That's fine as long as you come back to the exercise again and again until you've completed it. Perhaps you will not immediately remember something from your youngest years, but an adolescent memory is uppermost on your mind. Push yourself to access the earlier years, but don't get hung up if defining childhood moments don't surface. Keep going. You can come back to the earlier time after you've explored some of the later experiences. The life stories you're about to tell are important because they have had consequences in your life. They deserve your full concentration and focus. Promise yourself now that you'll care enough about yourself to do this right!

Defining Moment #1

1. Where are you at this moment?

2. How old are you?

3. Who is there with you, or who is supposed to be there with you?

4. What is happening that makes this moment so significant?

5. What emotions or changes of emotions are you experiencing (e.g., loneliness, anger, fear, confusion, joy, power, helplessness)?

6. How would you change this situation if you could?

7. What is your mental/physical experience?

    State of mind

Smells

Tastes

Touch

Happiness/sadness

Strength/weakness

8. If you could speak to someone at this moment, who would it be?

   What would you say?

9. What are you saying to yourself?

10. What do you need right now more than anything else?

Now bring yourself back to the present and answer the following questions.

1. How do you feel *now* about this defining moment?

2. What emotions are you having *now*?

3. What are you telling yourself about these events *today*?

4. What power and self-determination, if any, did you lose to this event, if it was a negative event? (If it was positive, what did you learn or gain?)

Defining Moment #2

1. Where are you at this moment?

2. How old are you?

3. Who is there with you, or who is supposed to be there with you?

4. What is happening that makes this moment so significant?

5. What emotions or changes of emotions are you experiencing (e.g., loneliness, anger, fear, confusion, joy, power, helplessness)?

6. How would you change this situation if you could?

7. What is your mental/physical experience?

State of mind

Smells

Tastes

Touch

Happiness/sadness

Strength/weakness

8. If you could speak to someone at this moment, who would it be?

    What would you say?

9. What are you saying to yourself?

10. What do you need right now more than anything else?

Now bring yourself back to the present and answer the following questions.

1. How do you feel *now* about this defining moment?

2. What emotions are you having *now*?

3. What are you telling yourself about these events *today*?

4. What power and self-determination, if any, did you lose to this event, if it was a negative event? (If it was positive, what did you learn or gain?)

Defining Moment #3

1. Where are you at this moment?

2. How old are you?

3. Who is there with you, or who is supposed to be there with you?

4. What is happening that makes this moment so significant?

5. What emotions or changes of emotions are you experiencing (e.g., loneliness, anger, fear, confusion, joy, power, helplessness)?

6. How would you change this situation if you could?

7. What is your mental/physical experience?

State of mind

Smells

Tastes

Touch

Happiness/sadness

Strength/weakness

8. If you could speak to someone at this moment, who would it be?

What would you say?

9. What are you saying to yourself?

10. What do you need right now more than anything else?

Now bring yourself back to the present and answer the following questions.

1. How do you feel *now* about this defining moment?

2. What emotions are you having *now*?

3. What are you telling yourself about these events *today*?

4. What power and self-determination, if any, did you lose to this event, if it was a negative event? (If it was positive, what did you learn or gain?)

Defining Moment #4

1. Where are you at this moment?

2. How old are you?

3. Who is there with you, or who is supposed to be there with you?

4. What is happening that makes this moment so significant?

5. What emotions or changes of emotions are you experiencing (e.g., loneliness, anger, fear, confusion, joy, power, helplessness)?

6. How would you change this situation if you could?

7. What is your mental/physical experience?

    State of mind

    Smells

    Tastes

    Touch

Happiness/sadness

Strength/weakness

8. If you could speak to someone at this moment, who would it be?

What would you say?

9. What are you saying to yourself?

10. What do you need right now more than anything else?

Now bring yourself back to the present and answer the following questions.

1. How do you feel *now* about this defining moment?

2. What emotions are you having *now*?

3. What are you telling yourself about these events *today*?

4. What power and self-determination, if any, did you lose to this event, if it was a negative event? (If it was positive, what did you learn or gain?)

Defining Moment #5

1. Where are you at this moment?

2. How old are you?

3. Who is there with you, or who is supposed to be there with you?

4. What is happening that makes this moment so significant?

5. What emotions or changes of emotions are you experiencing (e.g., loneliness, anger, fear, confusion, joy, power, helplessness)?

6. How would you change this situation if you could?

7. What is your mental/physical experience?

State of mind

Smells

Tastes

Touch

Happiness/sadness

Strength/weakness

8. If you could speak to someone at this moment, who would it be?

What would you say?

9. What are you saying to yourself?

10. What do you need right now more than anything else?

Now bring yourself back to the present and answer the following questions.

1. How do you feel *now* about this defining moment?

2. What emotions are you having *now*?

3. What are you telling yourself about these events *today*?

4. What power and self-determination, if any, did you lose to this event, if it was a negative event? (If it was positive, what did you learn or gain?)

Defining Moment #6

1. Where are you at this moment?

2. How old are you?

3. Who is there with you, or who is supposed to be there with you?

4. What is happening that makes this moment so significant?

5. What emotions or changes of emotions are you experiencing (e.g., loneliness, anger, fear, confusion, joy, power, helplessness)?

6. How would you change this situation if you could?

7. What is your mental/physical experience?

State of mind

Smells

Tastes

Touch

Happiness/sadness

Strength/weakness

8. If you could speak to someone at this moment, who would it be?

    What would you say?

9. What are you saying to yourself?

10. What do you need right now more than anything else?

Now bring yourself back to the present and answer the following questions.

1. How do you feel *now* about this defining moment?

2. What emotions are you having *now*?

3. What are you telling yourself about these events *today*?

4. What power and self-determination, if any, did you lose to this event, if it was a negative event? (If it was positive, what did you learn or gain?)

Defining Moment #7

1. Where are you at this moment?

2. How old are you?

3. Who is there with you, or who is supposed to be there with you?

4. What is happening that makes this moment so significant?

5. What emotions or changes of emotions are you experiencing (e.g., loneliness, anger, fear, confusion, joy, power, helplessness)?

6. How would you change this situation if you could?

7. What is your mental/physical experience?

State of mind

Smells

Tastes

Touch

Happiness/sadness

Strength/weakness

8. If you could speak to someone at this moment, who would it be?

    What would you say?

9. What are you saying to yourself?

10. What do you need right now more than anything else?

Now bring yourself back to the present and answer the following questions.

1. How do you feel *now* about this defining moment?

2. What emotions are you having *now*?

3. What are you telling yourself about these events *today*?

4. What power and self-determination, if any, did you lose to this event, if it was a negative event? (If it was positive, what did you learn or gain?)

Defining Moment #8

1. Where are you at this moment?

2. How old are you?

3. Who is there with you, or who is supposed to be there with you?

4. What is happening that makes this moment so significant?

5. What emotions or changes of emotions are you experiencing (e.g., loneliness, anger, fear, confusion, joy, power, helplessness)?

6. How would you change this situation if you could?

7. What is your mental/physical experience?

State of mind

Smells

Tastes

Touch

Happiness/sadness

Strength/weakness

8. If you could speak to someone at this moment, who would it be?

What would you say?

9. What are you saying to yourself?

10. What do you need right now more than anything else?

Now bring yourself back to the present and answer the following questions.

1. How do you feel *now* about this defining moment?

2. What emotions are you having *now*?

3. What are you telling yourself about these events *today*?

4. What power and self-determination, if any, did you lose to this event, if it was a negative event? (If it was positive, what did you learn or gain?)

Defining Moment #9

1. Where are you at this moment?

2. How old are you?

3. Who is there with you, or who is supposed to be there with you?

4. What is happening that makes this moment so significant?

5. What emotions or changes of emotions are you experiencing (e.g., loneliness, anger, fear, confusion, joy, power, helplessness)?

6. How would you change this situation if you could?

7. What is your mental/physical experience?

State of mind

Smells

Tastes

Touch

Happiness/sadness

Strength/weakness

8. If you could speak to someone at this moment, who would it be?

What would you say?

9. What are you saying to yourself?

10. What do you need right now more than anything else?

Now bring yourself back to the present and answer the following questions.

1. How do you feel *now* about this defining moment?

2. What emotions are you having *now*?

3. What are you telling yourself about these events *today*?

4. What power and self-determination, if any, did you lose to this event, if it was a negative event? (If it was positive, what did you learn or gain?)

Defining Moment #10

1. Where are you at this moment?

2. How old are you?

3. Who is there with you, or who is supposed to be there with you?

4. What is happening that makes this moment so significant?

5. What emotions or changes of emotions are you experiencing (e.g., loneliness, anger, fear, confusion, joy, power, helplessness)?

6. How would you change this situation if you could?

7. What is your mental/physical experience?

State of mind

Smells

Tastes

Touch

Happiness/sadness

Strength/weakness

8. If you could speak to someone at this moment, who would it be?

What would you say?

9. What are you saying to yourself?

10. What do you need right now more than anything else?

Now bring yourself back to the present and answer the following questions.

1. How do you feel *now* about this defining moment?

2. What emotions are you having *now*?

3. What are you telling yourself about these events *today*?

4. What power and self-determination, if any, did you lose to this event, if it was a negative event? (If it was positive, what did you learn or gain?)

CONNECTING THE DOTS

Look back over everything you've written. You've accomplished something critical in recalling and unpacking these memories. Have you left anything important out—either because it just came back to you, or because you've been avoiding talking about it? If so, work on it before you go on. Once you feel satisfied that you've done your best, continue.

Now that you know what your ten defining moments are, I want you to get a handle on these key pieces of your personal history. On the pages to come, use the questions provided to guide you through the process of understanding the impact these defining moments continue to have on your self-concept and life.

Begin by making a short-form list of the ten moments. This may help you as you look for common themes and connections. For the moment, ignore the "Emotion" and "When?" portion.

List Your Ten Defining Moments

1.

Emotion   When?

2.

Emotion   When?

3.

Emotion   When?

4.

Emotion   When?

5.

Emotion   When?

6.

Emotion   When?

7.

Emotion   When?

8.

Emotion   When?

9.

Emotion   When?

10.

Emotion   When?

Now go back to each event and label the emotional response the memory of that event produces in you. The emotional response may be hate or love, excitement or depression, comfort or anxiety, trust or suspicion, glee or sadness, a sense of security or fear. Or it may be something else. Record it in the space labeled "Emotion." When do you typically feel this emotion in the present? Write it out in the space labeled "When?"

WHAT YOUR DEFINING MOMENTS MEAN TO YOU TODAY
Refer again to the master list you've just made to complete the rest of this exercise.

Defining Moment #1

Describe this moment in one brief paragraph.

What change occurred in your self-concept as a result of this defining moment? Name the dimension(s) affected by this moment (for example: confidence, sense of security, hope, peace, ambition, joy, love, etc.).

Describe the "before" and "after" character of each dimension of your self-concept that was affected by this moment. Specifically, how were you different because of it?

Write a paragraph to describe the long-term residual effect of this defining moment. What qualities or lack of qualities have developed as a direct consequence of this event? How has it defined you?

Write down how and why you think the defining moment either clarified or distorted your authentic self. This may be a negative event with a negative effect, a negative event with a positive effect, a positive event with a negative effect, or a positive event with a positive effect. It may even be a mixed bag. Explore it and commit yourself to a position.

Review your interpretation of and reaction to the defining moment. Decide whether or not you believe your interpretation was and is accurate or inaccurate. Let time that has passed, objectivity, maturity, and experience help answer the question: "Has my interpretation of this defining moment been accurate? Or have I exaggerated or distorted it in some way?"

Write down whether this is something that you think you should keep or reject with regard to your concept of self. Include one paragraph as to why.

Defining Moment #2

Describe this moment in one brief paragraph.

What change occurred in your self-concept as a result of this defining moment? Name the dimension(s) affected by this moment (for example: confidence, sense of security, hope, peace, ambition, joy, love, etc.).

Describe the "before" and "after" character of each dimension of your self-concept that was affected by this moment. How were you different because of it?

Write a paragraph to describe the long-term residual effect of this defining moment. What qualities or lack of qualities have developed as a direct consequence of this event? How has it defined you?

Write down how and why you think the defining moment either clarified or distorted your authentic self. This may be a negative event with a negative effect, a negative event with a positive effect, a positive event with a negative effect, or a positive event with a positive effect. It may even be a mixed bag. Explore it and commit yourself to a position.

Review your interpretation of and reaction to the defining moment. Decide whether or not you believe your interpretation was and is accurate or inaccurate. Let time that has passed, objectivity, maturity, and experience help answer the question: "Has my interpretation of this defining moment been accurate? Or have I exaggerated or distorted it in some way?"

Write down whether this is something that you think you should keep or reject with regard to your concept of self. Include one paragraph as to why.

Defining Moment #3

Describe this moment in one brief paragraph.

What change occurred in your self-concept as a result of this defining moment? Name the dimension(s) affected by this moment (for example: confidence, sense of security, hope, peace, ambition, joy, love, etc.).

Describe the "before" and "after" character of each dimension of your self-concept that was affected by this moment. How were you different because of it.

Write a paragraph to describe the long-term residual effect of this defining moment. What qualities or lack of qualities have developed as a direct consequence of this event? How has it defined you?

Write down how and why you think the defining moment either clarified or distorted your authentic self. This may be a negative event with a negative effect, a negative event with a positive effect, a positive event with a negative effect, or a positive event with a positive effect. It may even be a mixed bag. Explore it and commit yourself to a position.

Review your interpretation of and reaction to the defining moment. Decide whether or not you believe your interpretation was and is accurate or inaccurate. Let time that has passed, objectivity, maturity, and experience help answer the question: "Has my interpretation of this defining moment been accurate? Or have I exaggerated or distorted it in some way?"

Write down whether this is something that you think you should keep or reject with regard to your concept of self. Include one paragraph as to why.

Defining Moment #4

Describe this moment in one brief paragraph.

What change occurred in your self-concept as a result of this defining moment? Name the dimension(s) affected by this moment (for example: confidence, sense of security, hope, peace, ambition, joy, love, etc.).

Describe the "before" and "after" character of each dimension of your self-concept that was affected by this moment. How were you different because of it?

Write a paragraph to describe the long-term residual effect of this defining moment. What qualities or lack of qualities have developed as a direct consequence of this event? How has it defined you?

Write down how and why you think the defining moment either clarified or distorted your authentic self. This may be a negative event with a negative effect, a negative event with a positive effect, a positive event with a negative effect, or a positive event with a positive effect. It may even be a mixed bag. Explore it and commit yourself to a position.

Review your interpretation of and reaction to the defining moment. Decide whether or not you believe your interpretation was and is accurate or inaccurate. Let time that has passed, objectivity, maturity, and experience help answer the question: "Has my interpretation of this defining moment been accurate? Or have I exaggerated or distorted it in some way?"

Write down whether this is something that you think you should keep or reject with regard to your concept of self. Include one paragraph as to why.

Defining Moment #5

Describe this moment in one brief paragraph.

What change occurred in your self-concept as a result of this defining moment? Name the dimension(s) affected by this moment (for example: confidence, sense of security, hope, peace, ambition, joy, love, etc.).

Describe the "before" and "after" character of each dimension of your self-concept that was affected by this moment. How were you different because of it?

Write a paragraph to describe the long-term residual effect of this defining moment. What qualities or lack of qualities have developed as a direct consequence of this event? How has it defined you?

Write down how and why you think the defining moment either clarified or distorted your authentic self. This may be a negative event with a negative effect, a negative event with a positive effect, a positive event with a negative effect, or a positive event with a positive effect. It may even be a mixed bag. Explore it and commit yourself to a position.

Review your interpretation of and reaction to the defining moment. Decide whether or not you believe your interpretation was and is accurate or inaccurate. Let time that has passed, objectivity, maturity, and experience help answer the question: "Has my interpretation of this defining moment been accurate? Or have I exaggerated or distorted it in some way?"

Write down whether this is something that you think you should keep or reject with regard to your concept of self. Include one paragraph as to why.

Defining Moment #6

Describe this moment in one brief paragraph.

What change occurred in your self-concept as a result of this defining moment? Name the dimension(s) affected by this moment (for example: confidence, sense of security, hope, peace, ambition, joy, love, etc.).

Describe the "before" and "after" character of each dimension of your self-concept that was affected by this moment. How were you different because of it?

Write a paragraph to describe the long-term residual effect of this defining moment. What qualities or lack of qualities have developed as a direct consequence of this event? How has it defined you?

Write down how and why you think the defining moment either clarified or distorted your authentic self. This may be a negative event with a negative effect, a negative event with a positive effect, a positive event with a negative effect, or a positive event with a positive effect. It may even be a mixed bag. Explore it and commit yourself to a position.

Review your interpretation of and reaction to the defining moment. Decide whether or not you believe your interpretation was and is accurate or inaccurate. Let time that has passed, objectivity, maturity, and experience help answer the question: "Has my interpretation of this defining moment been accurate? Or have I exaggerated or distorted it in some way?"

Write down whether this is something that you think you should keep or reject with regard to your concept of self. Include one paragraph as to why.

Defining Moment #7

Describe this moment in one brief paragraph.

What change occurred in your self-concept as a result of this defining moment? Name the dimension(s) affected by this moment (for example: confidence, sense of security, hope, peace, ambition, joy, love, etc.).

Describe the "before" and "after" character of each dimension of your self-concept that was affected by this moment. How were you different because of it?

Write a paragraph to describe the long-term residual effect of this defining moment. What qualities or lack of qualities have developed as a direct consequence of this event? How has it defined you?

Write down how and why you think the defining moment either clarified or distorted your authentic self. This may be a negative event with a negative effect, a negative event with a positive effect, a positive event with a negative effect, or a positive event with a positive effect. It may even be a mixed bag. Explore it and commit yourself to a position.

Review your interpretation of and reaction to the defining moment. Decide whether or not you believe your interpretation was and is accurate or inaccurate. Let time that has passed, objectivity, maturity, and experience help answer the question: "Has my interpretation of this defining moment been accurate? Or have I exaggerated or distorted it in some way?"

Write down whether this is something that you think you should keep or reject with regard to your concept of self. Include one paragraph as to why.

Defining Moment #8

Describe this moment in one brief paragraph.

What change occurred in your self-concept as a result of this defining moment? Name the dimension(s) affected by this moment (for example: confidence, sense of security, hope, peace, ambition, joy, love, etc.).

Describe the "before" and "after" character of each dimension of your self-concept that was affected by this moment. How were you different because of it.

Write a paragraph to describe the long-term residual effect of this defining moment. What qualities or lack of qualities have developed as a direct consequence of this event? How has it defined you?

Write down how and why you think the defining moment either clarified or distorted your authentic self. This may be a negative event with a negative effect, a negative event with a positive effect, a positive event with a negative effect, or a positive event with a positive effect. It may even be a mixed bag. Explore it and commit yourself to a position.

Review your interpretation of and reaction to the defining moment. Decide whether or not you believe your interpretation was and is accurate or inaccurate. Let time that has passed, objectivity, maturity, and experience help answer the question: "Has my interpretation of this defining moment been accurate? Or have I exaggerated or distorted it in some way?"

Write down whether this is something that you think you should keep or reject with regard to your concept of self. Include one paragraph as to why.

Defining Moment #9

Describe this moment in one brief paragraph.

What change occurred in your self-concept as a result of this defining moment? Name the dimension(s) affected by this moment (for example: confidence, sense of security, hope, peace, ambition, joy, love, etc.).

Describe the "before" and "after" character of each dimension of your self-concept that was affected by this moment. How were you different because of it.

Write a paragraph to describe the long-term residual effect of this defining moment. What qualities or lack of qualities have developed as a direct consequence of this event? How has it defined you?

Write down how and why you think the defining moment either clarified or distorted your authentic self. This may be a negative event with a negative effect, a negative event with a positive effect, a positive event with a negative effect, or a positive event with a positive effect. It may even be a mixed bag. Explore it and commit yourself to a position.

Review your interpretation of and reaction to the defining moment. Decide whether or not you believe your interpretation was and is accurate or inaccurate. Let time that has passed, objectivity, maturity, and experience help answer the question: "Has my interpretation of this defining moment been accurate? Or have I exaggerated or distorted it in some way?"

Write down whether this is something that you think you should keep or reject with regard to your concept of self. Include one paragraph as to why.

Defining Moment #10

Describe this moment in one brief paragraph.

What change occurred in your self-concept as a result of this defining moment? Name the dimension(s) affected by this moment (for example: confidence, sense of security, hope, peace, ambition, joy, love, etc.).

Describe the "before" and "after" character of each dimension of your self-concept that was affected by this moment. How were you different because of it.

Write a paragraph to describe the long-term residual effect of this defining moment. What qualities or lack of qualities have developed as a direct consequence of this event? How has it defined you?

Write down how and why you think the defining moment either clarified or distorted your authentic self. This may be a negative event with a negative effect, a negative event with a positive effect, a positive event with a negative effect, or a positive event with a positive effect. It may even be a mixed bag. Explore it and commit yourself to a position.

Review your interpretation of and reaction to the defining moment. Decide whether or not you believe your interpretation was and is accurate or inaccurate. Let time that has passed, objectivity, maturity, and experience help answer the question: "Has my interpretation of this defining moment been accurate? Or have I exaggerated or distorted it in some way?"

Write down whether this is something that you think you should keep or reject with regard to your concept of self. Include one paragraph as to why.

THE FRANKLIN T-CHART

Now go back to your list of the ten defining moments. Reviewing them as a whole, what has been the bottom-line effect on your concept of self, having lived through them? Would you say that your defining moments have affected your life positively or negatively? Use the T-chart provided here to review the effects. Don't stop filling up this T until you have thoroughly reviewed all of what you wrote in the preceding exercise. Then identify the *overall trend or pattern* among the ten events.

Positive Qualities	Negative Qualities

AND SO LIFE IS

You've done a considerable piece of work here. Take a moment before you move on to consider what you have learned. If you were to briefly describe to a close friend the most important discovery you have made so far, what would it be? Write it out here.

5 YOUR SEVEN CRITICAL CHOICES

Before you begin this portion of The Self Matters Companion, *read chapter 5 (pages 124–144) of* Self Matters: Creating Your Life from the Inside Out.

You have been looking back over the moments and events in your life that have had a lasting effect on your concept of self. It's essential to remember, however, that life is more than a series of events that happen *to* you. Your life demands an unceasing series of responses *from* you, and you make your responses in the form of choices. Whether you step up to the plate and choose boldly, or chicken out with the choice to *not* choose, you are actually choosing all the time. Some of your choices turn out really well. Others turn out to be disasters. Regardless of a choice's outcome for good or bad, it has the potential to powerfully affect your life. The older you become, the more power your choices carry—because the impact covers more and more ground, legally, morally, physically, financially, and socially.

Unlike the defining moments of your life, some of which were certainly outside of your control, the choices you have made and continue to make are 100 percent your responsibility. This doesn't mean that you know at the time what the possible consequences will or can be. It does mean that you and you alone make the ultimate choice about what you do or do not do, think or do not think, be or do not be.

The exercise that follows has two goals:

- to **identify the seven most critical choices** in your life;
- to **determine how your self-concept has been shaped** by the results of those choices.

Some of your choices and your internal responses to them have created major results that have caused distortions and defects in your self-concept and your interactions with the world. Yet you may not even remember the choices that got you where you are today. Your goal here is to recall critical choices and reconnect them in your understanding to their long-term results in your life.

First of all, I want you to think in terms of **what** you chose. Use the following list of life dimensions or categories to stimulate your thinking. There are many different arenas in your life, and you've made choices in all of them. You don't have to restrict yourself to this list, of course—if you think of another category that is important in your life, add it. Remember, too, that you should not feel compelled to draw a critical choice from each of the dimensions listed. One or another may or may not be relevant to this exercise. The list is provided just to help, not to define.

Personal Life
Physical Life
Professional Life
Family
Education
Spiritual Fulfillment
Social Life
Relationships

Think, too, in terms of **when**. Recall the various age brackets that you used as you considered the ten defining moments of your life. Again, you may discover a critical choice in nearly all of the categories or you may not. The breakdown is intended to help you dig more deeply than what occurs to you quickly.

Ages 1 to 5
Ages 6 to 12
Ages 13 to 20
Ages 21 to 38
Ages 39 to 55
Ages 56 and beyond

It may also be of help for you to consider **why** you chose as you did. What factors came into play when you were faced with a choice? As you search for your seven critical choices, keep in mind that you, like all humans, have certain motivations and needs that drive your choices from moment to moment. Experts have identified a hierarchy of human needs that seem to be generally present in all people. You satisfy the most basic needs first. As those are met, your needs become more sophisticated and refined. The needs, from most basic to most sophisticated, fall something like this:

- Survival
- Security
- Self-Esteem
- Love
- Self-Expression
- Intellectual Fulfillment, or
- Spiritual Fulfillment

Keep the **what, when,** and **why** of your choices in mind as you exercise your power of memory to discover these critical choices.

SEVEN CRITICAL CHOICES

What are the seven choices that have most profoundly shaped your outlook on life? You may find that it helps you identify these choices to go back to the exercises concerning your defining moments. Any of those defining moments could easily be a time when you made a choice that shaped your life view. Like the other exercises you have done, this examination of your critical choices requires privacy, quiet, a lack of distraction, and a comfortable place to sit a while. Do yourself the honor of treating this time of reflection seriously. You deserve the opportunity to make a positive impact on your life. Take this opportunity and do it right!

Critical Choice #1

Age bracket in which I made it

1. What was the choice? Write a sentence that describes it.

2. Why did you make it? Write a paragraph that describes what prompted this choice. Identify as many factors as you can recall.

3. What alternatives did you give up by making this choice? Write a paragraph that describes the "cost" of the choice you made.

4. Where were you, in terms of your self-concept, immediately *before* this choice, and what was your self-concept *after* this choice? What aspect or dimension of your self-concept was involved in or was affected by the choice? Write your observations down.

5. Write a paragraph to describe the long-term residual effect of this critical choice.

6. Write down how and why you think the critical choice either clarified or distorted your authentic self.

7. Review your interpretation of and reaction to the critical choice. Decide whether or not you believe your interpretation and whether it was and is accurate or inaccurate. Ask yourself: "Has my interpretation of this critical choice been accurate? Have I exaggerated or distorted it in some way?"

Critical Choice #2

Age bracket in which I made it

1. What was the choice? Write a sentence that describes it.

2. Why did you make it? Write a paragraph that describes what prompted this choice. Identify as many factors as you can recall.

3. What alternatives did you give up by making this choice? Write a paragraph that describes the "cost" of the choice you made.

4. Where were you, in terms of your self-concept, immediately *before* this choice, and what was your self-concept *after* this choice? What aspect or dimension of your self-concept was involved in or was affected by the choice? Write your observations down.

5. Write a paragraph to describe the long-term residual effect of this critical choice.

6. Write down how and why you think the critical choice either clarified or distorted your authentic self.

7. Review your interpretation of and reaction to the critical choice. Decide whether or not you believe your interpretation and whether it was and is accurate or inaccurate. Ask yourself: "Has my interpretation of this critical choice been accurate? Have I exaggerated or distorted it in some way?"

Critical Choice #3

Age bracket in which I made it

1. What was the choice? Write a sentence that describes it.

2. Why did you make it? Write a paragraph that describes what prompted this choice. Identify as many factors as you can recall.

3. What alternatives did you give up by making this choice? Write a paragraph that describes the "cost" of the choice you made.

4. Where were you, in terms of your self-concept, immediately *before* this choice, and what was your self-concept *after* this choice? What aspect or dimension of your self-concept was involved in or was affected by the choice? Write your observations down.

5. Write a paragraph to describe the long-term residual effect of this critical choice.

6. Write down how and why you think the critical choice either clarified or distorted your authentic self.

7. Review your interpretation of and reaction to the critical choice. Decide whether or not you believe your interpretation and whether it was and is accurate or inaccurate. Ask yourself: "Has my interpretation of this critical choice been accurate? Have I exaggerated or distorted it in some way?"

Critical Choice #4

Age bracket in which I made it

1. What was the choice? Write a sentence that describes it.

2. Why did you make it? Write a paragraph that describes what prompted this choice. Identify as many factors as you can recall.

3. What alternatives did you give up by making this choice? Write a paragraph that describes the "cost" of the choice you made.

4. Where were you, in terms of your self-concept, immediately *before* this choice, and what was your self-concept *after* this choice? What aspect or dimension of your self-concept was involved in or was affected by the choice? Write your observations down.

5. Write a paragraph to describe the long-term residual effect of this critical choice.

6. Write down how and why you think the critical choice either clarified or distorted your authentic self.

7. Review your interpretation of and reaction to the critical choice. Decide whether or not you believe your interpretation and whether it was and is accurate or inaccurate. Ask yourself: "Has my interpretation of this critical choice been accurate? Have I exaggerated or distorted it in some way?"

Critical Choice #5

Age bracket in which I made it

1. What was the choice? Write a sentence that describes it.

2. Why did you make it? Write a paragraph that describes what prompted this choice. Identify as many factors as you can recall.

3. What alternatives did you give up by making this choice? Write a paragraph that describes the "cost" of the choice you made.

4. Where were you, in terms of your self-concept, immediately *before* this choice, and what was your self-concept *after* this choice? What aspect or dimension of your self-concept was involved in or was affected by the choice? Write your observations down.

5. Write a paragraph to describe the long-term residual effect of this critical choice.

6. Write down how and why you think the critical choice either clarified or distorted your authentic self.

7. Review your interpretation of and reaction to the critical choice. Decide whether or not you believe your interpretation and whether it was and is accurate or inaccurate. Ask yourself: "Has my interpretation of this critical choice been accurate? Have I exaggerated or distorted it in some way?"

Critical Choice #6

Age bracket in which I made it

1. What was the choice? Write a sentence that describes it.

2. Why did you make it? Write a paragraph that describes what prompted this choice. Identify as many factors as you can recall.

3. What alternatives did you give up by making this choice? Write a paragraph that describes the "cost" of the choice you made.

4. Where were you, in terms of your self-concept, immediately *before* this choice, and what was your self-concept *after* this choice? What aspect or dimension of your self-concept was involved in or was affected by the choice? Write your observations down.

5. Write a paragraph to describe the long-term residual effect of this critical choice.

6. Write down how and why you think the critical choice either clarified or distorted your authentic self.

7. Review your interpretation of and reaction to the critical choice. Decide whether or not you believe your interpretation and whether it was and is accurate or inaccurate. Ask yourself: "Has my interpretation of this critical choice been accurate? Have I exaggerated or distorted it in some way?"

Critical Choice #7

Age bracket in which I made it

1. What was the choice? Write a sentence that describes it.

2. Why did you make it? Write a paragraph that describes what prompted this choice. Identify as many factors as you can recall.

3. What alternatives did you give up by making this choice? Write a paragraph that describes the "cost" of the choice you made.

4. Where were you, in terms of your self-concept, immediately *before* this choice, and what was your self-concept *after* this choice? What aspect or dimension of your self-concept was involved in or was affected by the choice? Write your observations down.

5. Write a paragraph to describe the long-term residual effect of this critical choice.

6. Write down how and why you think the critical choice either clarified or distorted your authentic self.

7. Review your interpretation of and reaction to the critical choice. Decide whether or not you believe your interpretation and whether it was and is accurate or inaccurate. Ask yourself: "Has my interpretation of this critical choice been accurate? Have I exaggerated or distorted it in some way?"

ANOTHER LOOK AT YOUR CHOICES

Take some time to go back and read through what you've just done. Your work in remembering and evaluating your critical choices is an important step in retrieving the history of your self-concept, and you will want to think over both what you have written and what it means to you today. What was most surprising to you as you remembered and wrote about your seven critical choices? Describe in writing what surprised you, and explain why it was surprising.

6 YOUR FIVE PIVOTAL PEOPLE

Before you begin this portion of The Self Matters Companion, *read chapter 6 (pages 145–156) of* Self Matters: Creating Your Life from the Inside Out.

It continues to amaze me that people devote so great a part of their life energy to denying who they are. They try to be so many things to so many people that they wear themselves out, drive themselves to illness and breakdown, and end up in a tragic disconnect from what and who matters most to them.

This journey you and I have undertaken together is all about getting back to who you really are. It's all about learning how to be your own best friend and greatest advocate, instead of your own worst enemy. It's all about understanding the expectations and demands of others in the context of your own hopes and dreams, talents and temperament, and coming out of these relationships with your authenticity intact.

In order to do that, however, you need to get real about the people who have "helped" you get where you are today. Whoever they are, these pivotal people have had or are having a huge impact on the formation and content of your self-concept. They have the power to mightily affect whether your life truly reflects your core self or some fictional self that has crowded the authentic you out of the picture.

Keep in mind that you have encountered probably hundreds or even thousands of individuals in your lifetime. Yet only a handful of those people have left an indelible mark on your life and self-concept. It is that handful that I want you to focus on now. You need first to identify the five people who have been most pivotal in determining your concept of self. You then need to examine in detail the role each has played. It's only when you come to grips with the reality of this that you can begin to deal with the effects in your life.

Remember, as well, that your pivotal people may include those who have made a powerfully positive impact on your experience at a critical moment or over an important period of time in your life. Just as certainly, they may include individuals whose negative impact resulted in a poisoning or distortion of your concept of self. They may include people whom you've known all your life or have just met. They may be individuals who are close to you or are relative strangers to you.

PEOPLE YOU HAVE KNOWN

Let's begin with the bigger picture. It's sometimes too easy to zero in on a certain few people in your life who show up a lot, and then assume that they must be the "pivotal" people. In uncovering the sources of development and distortion in your concept of self, however, there may be hidden pain or anxiety that generally keeps some of your personal history more deeply buried. So start by making a "master list" of individuals you remember from your life. Look back over the list of categories and age brackets in chapter 5 to stimulate your memory. You have known many more than fifty people by name in your lifetime. All I'm asking is that you come up with fifty, and there may even be one or two among them whose name you don't know! The easy ones are family and close friends. But don't forget teachers and religious leaders, coaches, employers or colleagues, neighbors or community leaders, people in the news, or even the local librarian. You may be surprised, as you revisit different times in your life, what comes to mind as you reconnect your memories to specific individuals.

Use this page to list at least fifty people you remember.

1.   3.

2.   4.

5.	28.
6.	29.
7.	30.
8.	31.
9.	32.
10.	33.
11.	34.
12.	35.
13.	36.
14.	37.
15.	38.
16.	39.
17.	40.
18.	41.
19.	42.
20.	43.
21.	44.
22.	45.
23.	46.
24.	47.
25.	48.
26.	49.
27.	50.

YOUR TOP TWENTY

From your list above, pick out the twenty who had the most influence in your life. These are people whom you not only remember, but have felt an effect from. If you were a pond, which of the fifty people you recalled would you say caused at least a ripple? List them here, along with a brief description of the role they played or are playing in your life.

1. Name   Role

2. Name   Role

3. Name	Role
4. Name	Role
5. Name	Role
6. Name	Role
7. Name	Role
8. Name	Role
9. Name	Role
10. Name	Role
11. Name	Role
12. Name	Role
13. Name	Role
14. Name	Role
15. Name	Role
16. Name	Role
17. Name	Role
18. Name	Role
19. Name	Role
20. Name	Role

Look back over the people you've chosen. Is there someone important whom you have left off the list? If so, add that person now.

YOUR FIVE PIVOTAL PEOPLE

Now let's get down to the real wavemakers in your experience. Who are the five pivotal people in your life? Who are the five people who shaped the self-concept that controls your life today, both positive and negative? Who has written on the "slate of you"? Remember: Your pivotal people are complicated people, just like you. None of them is 100 percent negative or 100 percent positive, and their effect on your self-concept may not exactly match your overall estimation of them as individuals. Question your assumptions about the nature of each person's effect on you.

To help you do an honest job of this, go back and read over what you wrote about your defining moments, in chapter 4, and your critical choices, in chapter 5. Even if you don't locate a pivotal person as a player in these important events and decisions, you may at least see connections that lead you to identify those individuals who have been pivotal. Your master list and your "top twenty" list above should also be a help to you. Once you've identified the five pivotal people in the spaces provided below, answer the questions that follow each name. This is an essential part of the process, so don't skip it. Make sure that you give yourself adequate time and privacy to do this exercise. Exercise your right to privacy, and tell it like it is on these pages. Your honesty now is critical to restoring an authentic self-concept.

Pivotal Person #1

Name:

Describe the actions of this person you now see as pivotal in your life. Include as much detail as you can, concentrating on the person's conduct or behavior as it relates to you and your self-concept. Make your description as concrete as possible; use action verbs that will help you "see" what happened as though you were there right now.

Describe this person's influence in your life. You have pinpointed particulars about conduct or behavior from this person that made a pivotal difference in the concept you now have of yourself. What specific effects did it have in your life? What consequences flow from the pivotal person directly to your present-day self?

Pivotal Person #2

Name:

Describe the actions of this person that you now see as pivotal in your life.

What specific effects did this person's actions have in your life? What consequences flow from the pivotal person directly to your present-day self?

Pivotal Person #3

Name:

Describe the actions of this person that you now see as pivotal in your life.

What specific effects did this person's actions have in your life? What consequences flow from the pivotal person directly to your present-day self?

Pivotal Person #4

Name:

Describe the actions of this person that you now see as pivotal in your life.

What specific effects did this person's actions have in your life? What consequences flow from the pivotal person directly to your present-day self?

Pivotal Person #5

Name:

Describe the actions of this person that you now see as pivotal in your life.

What specific effects did this person's actions have in your life? What consequences flow from the pivotal person directly to your present-day self?

WHAT ABOUT YOU?

You know what I'm about to ask. Were *you* on your list of pivotal people? Maybe, when you read chapter 6 of *Self Matters,* you realized that you *ought* to have a pivotal place in your own self-concept. Would you have thought of you if you hadn't read about it? If not, why not? Take some time to review what you've written about the pivotal people above.

What positive effects did you discover that had been generated in you as a result of your five pivotal people?

Describe yourself as a pivotal person in your own life *as you would like to be.* What can you imagine happening in you and for you as a result of being the top person on your list of your pivotal people? What would you gain emotionally, psychologically, physically, and behaviorally? Give time to this question and write out as complete a description as you can. Then spell out the results as you hope they would be.

7 LOCUS OF CONTROL

Before you begin this portion of The Self Matters Companion, *read the* "Introduction to Internal Factors" *section and chapter 7 (pages 156–182) of* Self Matters: Creating Your Life from the Inside Out.

The "Why?" question looms large in a human life. We want to know what causes the events and circumstances that affect our lives and the lives of the people around us. We don't have to be taught to ask "Why?" or "Who?" It's one of those questions that pops out of our mouths as soon as we learn to talk. We drive our parents to distraction with it when we're toddlers. It comes naturally, and we keep asking it throughout our lifetime, moment to moment, day to day.

Your **locus of control** has to do with where you tend to assign blame, credit, or cause for the events of your life—it is your internal default answer to the question "Why?" Your locus of control developed in your childhood and fell into a pattern of some kind as you responded to your unique set of circumstances and experiences. You may not have been aware that you operate with this "perceptual set" before you read about it in *Self Matters*. The wonderful thing about the knowledge you are gaining now is that once you know, you can change. And believe me, if your locus of control is keeping you out of the driver's seat of your own life, you want to change that. I'm going to help you.

The exercises that follow are designed to guide you in unearthing the way you interpret causes in your life. As always, your ability to understand and tune in to your authentic self depends on your willingness to get real about where you are right now and how you got there. Who or what is in charge of your life? Who is responsible for the results in your life? To whom or what do you look for answers or help when facing a challenge? Who is in control when things go wrong? Who gets the credit when things go right?

Don't try to figure out what the "right" answers to the questions are. There are no "right" answers. There are only answers that are *true about you* or *not true about you*. As you complete the exercises on the following pages, commit yourself right now to giving answers that are as true about you as you can make them. Let this be another leg of the wonderful journey you're taking toward a life that is true to your authentic self.

HEALTH CONTROL ATTRIBUTION QUESTIONNAIRE

I want you to begin by filling in both this and the following questionnaires. When you've done both, we'll look at what the results reveal about your locus of control.

For each statement below, decide how much you agree or disagree with it. Of the four answer choices, select the one that best expresses how you feel about the statement: If you agree totally, with no reservations, then circle (A); agree mostly, but with some reservations, (AS); disagree mostly, but with some reservations, (DS); or disagree completely, (D).

Section I	Agree	Agree Slightly	Disagree Slightly	Disagree
1. If I get sick, it is usually because I have not followed sound nutritional diets.	(A)	(AS)	(DS)	(D)
2. In order for me to get well from a disease, I will have to change my life habits and try hard.	(A)	(AS)	(DS)	(D)
3. I believe that good health is related to good life habits, such as exercise and stress management.	(A)	(AS)	(DS)	(D)

Section I	Agree	Agree Slightly	Disagree Slightly	Disagree
4. I believe that if I need to get well, I need to take responsibility for getting well.	(A)	(AS)	(DS)	(D)
5. Whether or not I get well is based on my efforts, not on those of doctors or hospitals.	(A)	(AS)	(DS)	(D)

Section II

	Agree	Agree Slightly	Disagree Slightly	Disagree
6. The most important thing in getting well is having a smart doctor.	(A)	(AS)	(DS)	(D)
7. I depend on my health providers to be experts, and to take care of me so I will not get sick.	(A)	(AS)	(DS)	(D)
8. Either our or some other government agency is using some weapons that make us sick.	(A)	(AS)	(DS)	(D)
9. The real reason I get well is because I take the right medicine.	(A)	(AS)	(DS)	(D)
10. I have to depend on doctors for my health status. What they say is right.	(A)	(AS)	(DS)	(D)

Section III

	Agree	Agree Slightly	Disagree Slightly	Disagree
11. If I get sick, it is the luck of the draw that day.	(A)	(AS)	(DS)	(D)
12. I am very lucky if I do not get sick.	(A)	(AS)	(DS)	(D)
13. It is an accident if a person dies, because no one really knows when you are going to get sick.	(A)	(AS)	(DS)	(D)
14. If I get a cold, it is because I happened to run into some cold germs that day.	(A)	(AS)	(DS)	(D)
15. Life is based on chance and luck.	(A)	(AS)	(DS)	(D)

Don't stop to add up your score yet. Continue through the following questionnaire.

CONTROL FOR SELF QUESTIONNAIRE

Section I	Agree	Agree Slightly	Disagree Slightly	Disagree
1. If I do not know myself, it is because I have not taken the time to assess who I really am.	(A)	(AS)	(DS)	(D)
2. In order for me to understand myself, I will have to look at my life perceptions.	(A)	(AS)	(DS)	(D)
3. I believe that I have the power and talents to be the person I want to be.	(A)	(AS)	(DS)	(D)
4. I believe that if I want to become who I am, I have to answer these hard questions about myself.	(A)	(AS)	(DS)	(D)
5. Whether or not I can be my authentic self will depend on my honesty with myself.	(A)	(AS)	(DS)	(D)

Section II

	Agree	Agree Slightly	Disagree Slightly	Disagree
6. The most important thing in getting to who I am is to ask my friends.	(A)	(AS)	(DS)	(D)
7. I depend on my friends to be experts on who I am.	(A)	(AS)	(DS)	(D)
8. There are experts who will tell me what my authentic self is.	(A)	(AS)	(DS)	(D)
9. The real me is what others think I am.	(A)	(AS)	(DS)	(D)
10. I have to depend on others for my self-esteem and status. What they say is right.	(A)	(AS)	(DS)	(D)

Section III

	Agree	Agree Slightly	Disagree Slightly	Disagree
11. If I get depressed, it is the luck of the draw.	(A)	(AS)	(DS)	(D)
12. I am very lucky if I get what I want.	(A)	(AS)	(DS)	(D)
13. It is an accident if I win or lose.	(A)	(AS)	(DS)	(D)

Section III	Agree	Agree Slightly	Disagree Slightly	Disagree
14. If I get to be myself one day, it will be because somebody happened to feel sorry for me.	(A)	(AS)	(DS)	(D)
15. Life is based on chance and luck.	(A)	(AS)	(DS)	(D)

IDENTIFYING YOUR LOCUS OF CONTROL

Now you're ready to start assessing what these questionnaires tell you about your locus of control. Begin by using the formulas below to figure out your scores for each section of each of the questionnaires. Add up the number of similar answers in a section, then multiply them as indicated below for your total scores.

HEALTH CONTROL ATTRIBUTION SCORING

SECTION I: INTERNAL LOCUS OF CONTROL

# Agree	_____ × 8 =	_____
# Agree slightly	_____ × 4 =	_____
# Disagree slightly	_____ × 2 =	_____
# Disagree	_____ × 1 =	_____
	TOTAL	_____

If you scored:

5–12 very low attribution of your health to internal responsibilities

13–20 low attribution of your health to internal responsibilities

21–32 average attribution of your health to internal responsibilities

33–40 high attribution of your health to internal responsibilities

SECTION II: EXTERNAL LOCUS OF CONTROL

# Agree	_____ × 8 =	_____
# Agree slightly	_____ × 4 =	_____
# Disagree slightly	_____ × 2 =	_____

Disagree   _____ × 1 = _____
                                   TOTAL_____

If you scored:

    5–10   very low attribution of your health to external sources
    11–15   low attribution of your health to external sources
    16–21   average attribution of authentic self to external sources
    22–40   high attribution of authentic self to external sources

SECTION III: CHANCE LOCUS OF CONTROL

    # Agree   _____ ×8 = _____
    # Agree slightly   _____ × 4 = _____
    # Disagree slightly   _____ × 2 = _____
    # Disagree   _____ × 1 = _____
                                   TOTAL _____

If you scored:

    5–9   very low attribution of health to chance
    10–17   low attribution of health to chance
    18–25   average attribution of health to chance
    26–40   high attribution of health to chance

WHAT DO YOUR SCORES MEAN?

First of all, if your score falls in the **high end of the chance** style of perception, you consider yourself at the mercy of random factors, which probably makes you very passive about the management of your health. Your self-concept is characterized by powerlessness.

A **high score on the external** scale suggests that you are highly dependent on powers outside of yourself, whether they are people or things. You are probably too passive about your health management. You've created a vulnerable position for yourself by giving away your power.

A **higher internal score** is often productive, because you understand and act on the fact that most major health issues can be influenced by what you do or don't do. You have retained power over your health choices.

CONTROL FOR SELF SCORING

SECTION I: INTERNAL LOCUS OF CONTROL

# Agree	_____ × 8 =	_____
# Agree slightly	_____ × 4 =	_____
# Disagree slightly	_____ × 2 =	_____
# Disagree	_____ × 1 =	_____
	TOTAL	_____

If you scored:

5–20   low attribution of authentic self to internal source

21–32 average attribution of authentic self to internal sources

33–40 high attribution of authentic self to internal sources

SECTION II: EXTERNAL LOCUS OF CONTROL

# Agree	_____ × 8 =	_____
# Agree slightly	_____ × 4 =	_____
# Disagree slightly	_____ × 2 =	_____
# Disagree	_____ × 1 =	_____
	TOTAL	_____

If you scored:

5–15   low attribution of authentic self to external source

16–21 average attribution of authentic self to external sources

22–40 high attribution of authentic self to external sources

SECTION III: CHANCE LOCUS OF CONTROL

# Agree	_____ × 8 =	_____
# Agree slightly	_____ × 4 =	_____
# Disagree slightly	_____ × 2 =	_____
# Disagree	_____ × 1 =	_____
	TOTAL	_____

If you scored:

5–17   Low attribution of authentic self to chance

18–25 Average attribution of authentic self to chance

26–40 High attribution of authentic self to chance

WHAT DO YOUR SCORES MEAN ON THIS QUESTIONNAIRE?

If you scored in the **high classifications for internal** and in the **lower levels of chance,** then you take responsibility for positive change in your life. You can ask yourself hard questions that help you regain clarity and authenticity.

If you scored **highest on the external** scale, you need to figure out why you have given up your control of self. You need to go on the alert against falling into the classic "victim" role.

If you scored **highest on the chance** scale, you're sitting in bleachers when you should be out on the playing field. You need to decide right now, while you still have a life to live, that you are going to get actively involved in it.

WHOSE FAULT IS IT, ANYWAY?

Let's look at this in another way. Your life is full of consequences, or outcomes. Something happens, and something caused it to happen. Whether you realize it or not, every time you experience one of those consequences, you assign blame, credit, or at least cause. *Where* you tend to place blame, give credit, or assign cause is what locus of control is all about. You've done some fine work and found roughly how you perceive the source of power in your life. I want you to get a visual idea of where your locus of control falls on a range from *internal* to *chance* to *external.* The exercise that follows is designed to help you "see" your internal workings a little more clearly. But it will only help in that regard if you rate your responses as honestly as you possibly can. If one of the phrases below doesn't fit your life or situation exactly, rethink it in some way that makes it applicable to your experience. Then mark with an X the response that most closely matches where you would assign the primary responsibility for the outcome described.

When this happens, the responsible one is . . .	1 Mostly me	2 Luck of the draw	3 Mostly someone else
When my life partner (best friend) and I fight			
When I catch a cold			
When I persuade someone of my viewpoint			
When I get a promotion			
When I gain too much weight			
When I do a job poorly			
When I make a new friend			
When I spend too much			
When I "fall off the wagon"			
When a loved one dies			
When I have a "fender bender"			
When I "sound like my mother/father"			
When I'm late for an appointment			
When I'm betrayed by a friend			
When I ace a task			
When I'm chosen to lead a group			
When I lose my temper			
When I miss a deadline			
When my car breaks down			
When I treat someone negatively			
TOTAL	1.	2.	3.

Add up the X's in each column. The pie chart below is divided into twenty slices. You're going to turn this pie into your personalized **Locus of Control Chart.**

- Using a pen, fill in one slice for each X that you marked in Column 1. For example, if you totaled eight X's in Column 1, you should fill in eight pie slices (choose eight that are connected to one another) and end up with a pen-colored wedge that is eight slices wide.

- Using a pencil this time, do the same for Column 2. For every X in Column 2, shade a slice of the pie with your pencil. You should now have one pen-colored wedge and one pencil-shaded wedge.

- The remaining slices with no color on them should equal the number of X's in Column 3.

Look at the pie. If you're like most people, it isn't just one color. But you may begin to get a better idea, proportionately, of who or what you feel is responsible for what happens in your life. Whichever wedge is largest represents where your locus of control tends to be. Whichever is smallest represents the last source of power you tend to ascribe to your life.

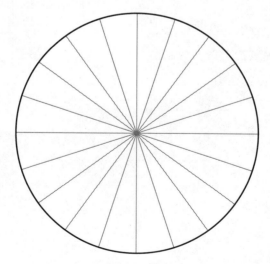

WHERE DO YOU FIT?

By now, you should have a clear understanding of which of the three styles of interpreting and responding to events in your life best describes your approach. Let's get more specific. Think back over the last week. I want you to identify five events in your life that occurred in the last week and describe them in the spaces provided below.

1.

2.

3.

4.

5.

For each of the events you've just described, answer the following questions:

- Where did you assign responsibility for that event? Did you see yourself as responsible? Did you interpret the event as caused by someone or something other than yourself? Or did you see it as a random, chance event?

1.

2.

3.

4.

5.

- On reflection, do you think your locus of control in each event was accurate? Have you accepted a victim role instead of accepting responsibility for something you could have changed? Have you taken credit or blame for something that, in fact, is outside of your control? Or did you inappropriately shrug off responsibility in the name of luck?

1.

2.

3.

4.

5.

Give this exercise some quality time. The more you see how your locus of control affects the way you live and choose, the better able you will be to tune in to your authentic self and make changes that need to be made.

WHAT'S YOUR STYLE?

Your locus of control is critical to your concept of self and your ability to live an authentic life. Before we move on, restate in the space provided below what you have learned about yourself and your locus of control. Describe your typical style of interpreting the events in your life. Where are you now in this regard? Where would you like to be a year from now?

8 INTERNAL DIALOGUE

Before you begin this portion of The Self Matters Companion, *read chapter 8 (pages 183–208) of* Self Matters: Creating Your Life from the Inside Out.

Your internal dialogue may be the loudest voice you hear most of your waking hours. Like your self-concept and your locus of control, it developed over years. It is the real-time, real-language conversation you have with yourself every moment of every day, and it has a profound effect on the way you perceive the events and choices in your life. It gives you feedback constantly, judging, assessing, warning you or chiding you, cheering you on, praising you, disapproving of you, painting a rosy picture, or sending messages of gloom and doom.

By now, I shouldn't have to say this again, but it bears repeating: If you want to return to your authentic self and live a life that will satisfy your deepest needs, you have to get real about your internal dialogue. Everyone, you included, is subject to distorting or missing the truth. Remember your defining moments, critical choices, and pivotal people. As you identified and evaluated those crucial elements of your life and self-concept, you began to see how many false messages and ideas have been introduced into your internal life over time. If you're honest with yourself, I'd bet that you admit that the loudest messages and ideas you've received have been negative, no matter how many positives were included in the mix. Negative messages—criticisms, condemnations, rejections—hurt, and humans are designed to pay attention to pain. The journey back to authenticity depends on you looking squarely at what you say to yourself and weeding out the false messages you've made part of your internal dialogue.

Keep in mind that as you talk to yourself, you undergo physiological changes that reflect the messages you are sending. You blush or grow pale, perspire or get chills, develop a racing heart or sink into depression. Your self-talk can drown out any and all alternative messages from the "outside," overriding valuable information that could help you avoid distorted perceptions, and subverting important input that could lead to success or keep you out of trouble. Because of this, the false messages can actually create self-fulfilling prophecies. You believe—despite all evidence to the contrary—that you are inadequate to make some important change or decision, and when the time comes, that negative message that you are sending yourself creates exactly what you don't want. You think it, do it, and become it.

It's time to change that dynamic. As you've seen throughout this study, in order to change, you need to know the truth of what you're dealing with. The exercises that follow are designed to help you tune in consciously to your internal dialogue, to hear what you are telling yourself, assess its source, and test its accuracy. Only then can you challenge the false messages and live more in accordance with your authentic self.

HOW DO YOU FEEL WHEN . . . ?

Let's take a look first at some of your "gut" reactions when you are dealing with others. Don't overthink this, but be as honest as you can. Listed below are a series of situations. Finish each of the sentences briefly, using as many descriptive terms as you can. Include emotions (sad, angry, hurt, happy, hopeful, scared, tense), physical reactions (tired, shaky, sweaty, hyped-up, weak-kneed, full of pep, headachy), and thoughts ("I can't do this," "this should be fun," "he doesn't like me," "she'll probably say no," "it's my fault").

1. When someone compliments my appearance, I . . .

2. When a family member criticizes something I do, I . . .

3. When I make a wrong turn on the road, I . . .

4. When I need to register a complaint with a business associate or vendor, I . . .

5. When a total stranger treats me badly, I . . .

6. When someone close to me successfully gets in shape, I . . .

7. When the service in a shop or restaurant is poor, I . . .

8. When someone does something special for me that they don't have to do, I . . .

9. When I forget to do something I promised to do, I . . .

10. When my boss asks me to redo something at work, I . . .

WHAT'S THE PAYOFF?

Now that you've taken a first look at some of your typical reactions, I want you to go back and give them a second look. Put a star (*) next to every statement you've written above that could be categorized, either partially or wholly, as a negative assessment of yourself. In other words, what negative self-talk are you throwing at yourself in these situations? Once you've identified the negative internal dialogue, use the spaces below to answer this question about each of the situations in which you put yourself in a negative light: What do you get out of reacting with self-criticism? This is what the payoff factor is all about.

The low self-esteem acted out in your internal dialogue can be a handy excuse for choosing not to change, not to challenge yourself, not to step up to the plate. What's the payoff for *you*?

1.

2.

3.

4.

5.

6.

7.

8.

9.

10.

TAKING INVENTORY

What you've done is a start. Now it's time to go on the alert more broadly in regard to your internal dialogue. You need to find out exactly what it is that you tell yourself throughout your days. Once you've identified the messages you are sending yourself, you'll be able to evaluate those messages for authenticity and accuracy. You'll also have the information you need to change the internal dialogue in ways that promote the life you want to have and the person you are capable of being.

EXERCISE 1: A DAY IN THE LIFE

Pick a day for this exercise that is as close to typical as possible. Plan to carry a small notebook and pen with you everywhere you go for the entire day. Then make a series of appointments with yourself. Every two hours or so, stop whatever you're doing for just a few moments and write down what you've been telling yourself about the following topics:

- your appearance
- the work that you've been doing for the past two hours
- your job, more generally
- your intelligence
- your competence
- your skills and abilities
- your worth

You may find that it's easier to simply jot things down as they occur to you, rather than waiting for appointed times. That's fine, as long as you make a point of doing it regularly. At the end of the day, transfer your notes to the space below or attach them here.

EXERCISE 2: PRESENTING . . .

I want you to put your imagination to work. Imagine that you have an important presentation to make in front of the person you work for, as well as several of your coworkers and clients. It's the night before your presentation and you're lying in bed, in the dark, thinking about what you are about to do. What are you saying to yourself?

Take enough time to think this through honestly and thoroughly. If such a scenario is too far removed from your personal experience, think of a similar situation in which you are in the spotlight, with important people in your audience. Visualize yourself in that situation—what you would wear, where you would stand, what you might be saying. There's no question that as the presentation time neared, you'd be thinking about all these things and more. So what would you be saying? Write down as much of this internal conversation as you can.

EXERCISE 3: WHAT ARE YOUR THEMES?

Now look back over what you wrote in the previous two exercises. What common themes or threads do you see in your responses? Describe the common features below.

EXERCISE 4: HOW DO YOU FEEL?

Now read over your responses to Exercises 1 and 2 again. This time, pay attention to the overall tone or mood of your internal dialogue. Note whether you are optimistic or pessimistic, and whether in either case your mood reflects reality or feelings or both. Look for whether you are upbeat or defeatist and self-condemning. Consider, as well, whether you tend to pump yourself up with a self-con job. Perhaps you are at times especially harsh or critical. Describe in writing what tone you find.

Go back and circle any language in the first two exercises that you think illustrates either especially positive or especially negative internal dialogue. If you find either of these extremes, what specifically are they in reference to?

Positive

Negative

EXERCISE 5: WHAT CONTROLS YOUR LIFE?

Go back to chapter 8 and review what you wrote regarding your locus of control. With that in mind, return again to Exercises 1 and 2 of this chapter. What does this most recent writing tell you about where you assign responsibility for the events and choices in your life? Write it in the space provided here.

Does your writing on internal dialogue add any new insights to your understanding of your locus of control? If so, in what regard?

EXERCISE 6: WHAT KIND OF A FRIEND ARE YOU TO YOU?

Having reviewed the sorts of messages you are whispering in your own ear all the time, you are better equipped to evaluate whether you promote authenticity in your life or inhibit it with toxic messages. Answer the question: What kind of friend are you to yourself? Imagine that someone other than you were saying the things you say to yourself. What kind of friend would that person be? Describe yourself in writing as a friend to you.

IN CONVERSATION WITH YOURSELF

What have you discovered about your internal dialogue as you've responded to the exercises in this section? Write a short paragraph that sums up what you've learned in a way that you could communicate to another person.

If you could change anything in your internal dialogue, what would it be? Describe what you would change and how you would like to change it.

9 LABELS

Before you begin this portion of The Self Matters Companion *read chapter 9 (pages 209–223) of* Self Matters: Creating Your Life from the Inside Out.

The world loves labels. With labels, individuals can be kept in their societal place. But labels are serious business when it comes to self-concept. They are one of the ways that your authenticity is attacked, both by others and by you, and they lie at the heart of the fictional self you develop. Your parents may have bestowed many of the labels you continue to believe, or it may have been schoolmates, teachers, coaches, or employers. You may have accumulated self-labels over time in response to your own missteps. The source ultimately matters less than the fact of the labels' ongoing power to influence your life and self-concept. You're aiming for authenticity. As long as labels are allowed to remain unchallenged in your view of you, however, you are subverting your own efforts to reclaim the real you.

The exercises that follow are designed to:

- help you understand and acknowledge that you do indeed carry labels about yourself around with you;
- help you challenge whether the labels "fit" who you authentically are; and
- help you confront the impact the labels have had on your concept of self.

Your labels may apply externally, as when you are identified with the job you do or the function you fulfill. But remember that at the same time, you are buying into labels that reflect judgments you or others have made about your worth, abilities, or qualities. The labels, whatever their nature, create artificial limits in your view of yourself and, as a result, your choices and behavior. They become the boundaries you believe you cannot cross.

As you prepare to complete the following exercises, go back to chapter 8 and review what you recorded in the section about internal dialogue. With a clearer understanding of what labels are and how they function in your concept of self, you may now be able to see labels in your self-talk, either overt or implied. Read through what you wrote, and ask yourself: "If this is the way I talk to myself, what labels must I have accepted as true about me?" As you continue through this section, be alert, as well, for any labeling that may have been offered kindly, but nevertheless diminished your sense of yourself. Push yourself to uncover the most deeply buried labels and challenge the most convincing labels. Labels do not serve authenticity because they limit your sense of what's possible and distort your perceptions of self. It's time to bring your real self into focus. Give this section your best time and attention.

WHAT'S IN A NAME?

You may not think a lot about the most obvious label you carry, your given name. But it is often the first way that you identify yourself to others. Write your name here.

Look at your name. Does your name have any special meaning to you? Maybe you've looked it up in a "book of names," or you've heard family stories of what it means to your parents or others. If so, what is its significance?

Do you believe that the people in your family or community associate any particular traits, habits, or reputation with your name? If so, what specifically is associated with your name?

You may, without being conscious of it, have absorbed a concept of yourself from the meaning of or associations with your name. Chances are, though, that the name you were given at birth is not the only name you answer to. In our world, nicknames are as prominent as names. Many stars in sports, business, and show business become as well or better known by their nicknames than they are by their given names. Has anyone ever nicknamed you? Were there pet names or nicknames used by family members, close friends, teachers or coaches, schoolmates or work colleagues? If so, what were/are your nicknames or pet names?

Consider any nickname or pet name you recorded above. How did you come to be given that nickname? What did/does it mean to you?

The naming of a child is treated very seriously in some communities. Some people believe that a name's meaning (it may, for example, mean wisdom, beauty, strength, or swiftness) is actually invested in the individual who is given that name, either mystically or through the power of suggestion. Given what we know about the potency of a label, such an idea doesn't seem all that farfetched. Some cultures even enact a rite of passage that involves giving a new name to an individual when he or she comes of age. In some cases, the individual is given responsibility for choosing the new name for him or herself.

Imagine that you are a member of such a community. It is now your job to choose a two-part name for yourself. The first part of the name should be a descriptive word (for example: beautiful, soaring, strong, wise, running, wild, patient, sitting, falling, etc.). The second part of the name should be a noun (an animal name—bull, eagle, frog, bear, lion, pigeon, etc.; a flower or plant name—rose, oak, tumbleweed, chestnut, lily, cactus, etc.; or an object—rock, mountain, river, pebble, garden, fire, etc.). If you were to choose a name that describes who you are today, what would you choose?

If nothing else, this exercise should highlight for you the variety of ways in which you receive and accept a name or label. I hope it also begins to show you how such names and labels can exert a powerful influence on who you become and what you choose to do with your life.

WHAT ARE YOUR LABELS?

Let me repeat that the world loves labels. There's no way you've grown up in the company of other people and avoided labels. What you need to do is identify what those labels are. You may see some of your labels as positive and some as negative. It's important to remember that *any* label is limiting, because you are not one thing. You are a multifaceted, unique person who has been given everything you need to make a rich, fulfilling life for yourself. Every time you buy into a label, you allow yourself to be boxed, as though you were simply a category as opposed to a vibrant, original human being. Labels come in different forms. To help you pinpoint your labels, I've given you several categories of labels below that may apply to you. Go through each category and write down every label you can think of from that category that you have received, starting as far back as you can remember. Your list will include some labels that you know had some influence on your self-concept and some that you have rejected.

Look for **relational labels:** first born, middle child, baby of the family, mother, father, single, divorcé(e), widow(er), lovable, unlovable, difficult, curmudgeon, moody, passionate, cold, overdramatic, PMS-y, your astrological sign, sensitive, jerk, hellion, and so on:

Look for **career or job labels:** boss, sidekick, lackey, gofer, loser, hound dog, go-getter, whiner, ball-buster, demander, hired help, climber, plodder, and so on:

Look for **talent/appearance labels:** jock, beauty queen, freak, geek, skinny, fat, plump, buff, weak, short, bad-skinned, baldy, stacked, clumsy, graceful, ugly, inept, delicate, sickly, hopeless, and so on:

Look for **intellectual labels:** smart, brilliant, dumb, lazy, achiever, overachiever, underachiever, dimwit, flake, nerd, absentminded, brown-noser, and so on:

Look for **status or value labels:** second-class, privileged, wrong side of town, inferior, silver spoon, cool or uncool, rebel, bad, goody-goody, and so on:

LABELS FROM YOUR PARENTS

After you have listed every label you can remember in the preceding exercise, circle every label that you believe was **put on you by your parents.** Then copy the circled labels into the left-hand column below. Although many of the labels had their beginning so long ago that you can't remember when they first came to your attention, try to think back to the first time you felt their sting and what you were doing at the time. Use the chart below to record as much detail as possible for each label.

Label	First Time Mentioned	What You Were Doing

PARENTAL LABELS THAT LIVE ON

Go back over the chart you just completed. Which of the labels that you identified continue to affect your life today? Put a checkmark beside each one that continues to be relevant in some way. Below, write out how you see yourself operating on the belief that these labels are true today and still reflect you.

LABELS FROM OTHERS

Look again at the original list of labels you created. Which of those labels were you given by **people other than your parents?** In the chart below, record everything you can remember about who gave you each label, when you received this label, and what you were doing at the time.

Label	Given to You By	First Time Mentioned	What You Were Doing

LABELS FROM YOURSELF

It is now time for you to assess the ways in which you have accepted labels and made them your own. You need to give yourself the time and circumstances to really focus on this exercise, because the labels you give yourself are often the hardest to recognize. These are the labels that you took away from some event *as conclusions about yourself.* In others, you bit; you believed the label then and made it part of your self-concept so that you continue to believe it.

Identify each self-label in the left-hand column. In the middle column, record what the circumstances were when you received that label. In the right-hand column, pinpoint situations in which you identified with the label; that is, when you accepted the label as a true statement about you.

Label	The Situation When You First Received the Label	The Situations in Which You Have Believed that the Label Is a True Statement About You

IMAGINE THIS

Just to put this in perspective, imagine that you are a potential employer who has been handed your list of self-labels as a resumé. Write your impressions as a hiring agent of the person you have described with these labels. What do you think of this person? How accurate do you really think the labels are?

THE YOU THAT YOU CHOOSE

No matter how many labels you've bought into in the past, and regardless of the payoffs, you don't have to keep doing what you've done. The exercises you've just completed have given you valuable information. You know a whole lot more now than you did when you started. When you know better, you can do better. Early in this section, I asked you to name yourself as a way of describing who you are today. I want you to name yourself again, but instead of describing who you are right now, choose a name that describes who you would like to be a month or a year from now. This is not a new way to label yourself. Rather, it is an opportunity to focus on your authentic self. Describe the person *you look forward to being,* the person you really are when the fictional self is rejected and laid aside. Again, the first part of the name should be a descriptive word; the second should be a noun of your choice.

10 LIFE SCRIPTS

Before you begin this portion of The Self Matters Companion, *read chapter 10 (pages 224–249) of* Self Matters: Creating Your Life from the Inside Out.

You are now aware that you talk to yourself in a very influential way all the time. I hope that you are becoming better at tuning in to your self-talk and rejecting the false and defeatist notes that creep into your conversation with yourself. I want you to go even further. Your internal dialogue happens in real time at a speed that you can follow. But at a deeper level, you have a different kind of message that you play to yourself. It is a message that I call a *tape*—negative self-talk that you have overlearned by repeating and rehearsing it endlessly—and it plays at such lightning speed, you don't even know it's running. It is as automatic as breathing, and it exerts a powerful level of control over the way you perceive reality and respond to events and circumstances.

The problem with tapes is that they are based entirely on history. While your life goes on in the present, confronting you with an ever-changing range of people and experiences, your tapes are playing the same old messages, literally programming you to respond in ways that ignore current input and aim for a preaccepted outcome. How can you possibly live true to your authentic self when you've got those old judgments and limiting beliefs tying you to the fictions you've chosen to believe?

The good news is that you can slow the tapes down sufficiently to hear the messages you're sending yourself. Once you know what they are, you can choose to reject them. You can plant yourself firmly in the here and now and make choices based on facts.

The exercises that follow offer a variety of ways in which you can slow your tapes and scrutinize them. As you identify each tape and understand its source, you'll be able to see how it has contributed to the life script you have accepted, defining the roles you play in life, and creating the expectations and roles you impose on others. Be patient with yourself. Give yourself time and space to do this carefully. You are dealing with messages that have become second nature to you, and they will not automatically surface. You have to dig. But your efforts will be amply rewarded if you deal with yourself truthfully and stay with it. You *can* make a difference.

COMMON TAPES

You have tapes playing in the background of your life. Whether or not you know what they are, you can be sure that they're playing. It's important that you put yourself to the trouble of tuning in to them. As a beginning exercise, read the following statements. If a statement, or some close variation on it, rings true about you, circle T for true. In this case, I want you to change the statement right on the page in whatever way you need to in order to make it as accurate to your life as possible. If a statement has no ring of truth to your experience, circle F for false.

T   F   I will never have a good experience. My childhood was too unhappy, and I bring the unhappiness to every situation I'm in.

T   F   I'm no fun to be with. My family was so dysfunctional, we never learned how to have fun.

T   F   I'm so ugly. My face and body don't look anything like the faces and bodies of the people with lots of friends. I'll have to settle for being mostly alone.

T   F   My future will be like my past. I've always been unlucky and unproductive, and that won't ever change.

T	F	I should never expect to be successful. I never succeed. It isn't my destiny to succeed.
T	F	I have done some bad things in my life, and I can't be forgiven. I'll have to bear my guilt forever, and it will mean that things don't turn out well for me.
T	F	I am not worthy of people's best treatment. They will always disappoint me and hurt me.
T	F	I was abused as a child. All men will use me for what they want and be insensitive to how I feel.
T	F	My family was low class. I will be low class. There is nothing I can do to change that.
T	F	My father/mother was a loser. I will be a loser, regardless of what happens.
T	F	I am a leader. People look to me to be strong and to set an example. I must never show my weakness or ask for the help of others, for the rest of my life.
T	F	Laziness is a sin, so I should never relax.
T	F	My parents bungled their finances completely. I will never be able to handle money well. I'll always have to struggle.

There's no scoring on this little quiz. I simply want you to pay attention to the tapes above that have a familiar feel to them. Be on the alert for other such statements and ideas that may be part of your tapes. Because these tapes are faster than conscious thought and often at work without you knowing it, it's important when you do discover one of these negative tapes in your own thinking to write it down. It cannot work on you in the dark if you shine a light on it.

WHAT ARE YOUR FIXED BELIEFS?

If your tapes are the negative self-talk that has created your automatic responses to events in your life, your fixed beliefs are your stage director. They define your limits and roles, responsibilities and possibilities. They act as inhibitors to change and creativity. They become your predictors about your future and the outcomes of your choices. In fact, they dictate your choices. Understand that all this happens without your conscious awareness. When your fixed beliefs are in play, your past is in charge of your future.

I'm sure it is becoming clear to you that unidentified fixed beliefs do not put you on the path to a more authentic self and life. Instead, they anchor you to a fictional self that cheats you of a fulfilling, passionate life.

Let's scope out some of the fixed beliefs that may be holding you where you are. Read each phrase below, then finish it to make a complete sentence. If the beginning clause does not apply to your personal history, change it so that it does.

When my teacher seemed unhappy with me, it was because . . .

When I had my first car accident, it was because . . .

When I wasn't voted onto the student council, it was because . . .

When I failed the test, it was because . . .

When I wound up with the wrong person, it was because . . .

When I dropped out of high school/college/graduate school, it was because . . .

When I lost my job, it was because . . .

When my friend betrayed me, it was because . . .

Look over what you've just written. Did anything show up more than once? Do you see any themes? What fixed beliefs do you see at work in the above? Write them here.

I DIDN'T CHANGE BECAUSE . . .

Keep in mind that your fixed beliefs are often limiting beliefs. They keep you in your safety zone, even when that safety zone cheats you out of the best you could be, do, and have. Push yourself a little bit further now, and consider some specific limiting beliefs that may be playing on your tapes and running your life. Again, finish each sentence below. Give yourself time to think about times when you were in the situation described, and then spell out in detail why you responded as you did.

When I was given less than I hoped for, I didn't do anything about it because . . .

When I was presented with a challenge that I'd never experienced before, I chose not to try because . . .

When I see someone with something I don't have but wish I did, I don't make changes that would help me get it because . . .

When I have been cheated out of what I paid for at a restaurant/shop/show, I have failed to complain or insist on my due because . . .

When I am treated as the second person in a relationship, the one who functions as the supporter all the time, I do nothing to change that because . . .

All the situations above deal with ways in which you can limit your potential and your options. There may be other situations in your life in which the same thing happens. Just as you've done above, you need to explain to yourself *why*. Until you know that, you will continue to shortchange yourself. Go over your responses as you did in the previous exercise and look for any common themes to your choices. If you were asked to sum up in one sentence what keeps you from making changes, what would you say? Write it here.

IDENTIFYING YOUR OWN TAPES

I want you to start slowing down your tapes so you can hear them and analyze them. In the following exercises, you'll need to be patient and attentive. If you give yourself the time and attention to do so, you can discover what you believe at different times in your life and how those beliefs affect what you are and do. Make no assumptions. Jump to no conclusions. Really listen to yourself and write down your reflections.

MEETING THE BEST
Assume that you are about to meet someone for whom you have great respect. Imagine a celebrity, a very rich and powerful person, or someone whose values and beliefs you hold in the highest regard. As you anticipate this meeting, question yourself very carefully and answer with as much honesty and thoroughness as you can. Acknowledge every response you feel regarding the coming meeting, no matter how good or bad it makes you feel about yourself. In *completely specific terms,* write down what you are telling yourself.

DAILY DIARY
Every morning for the next week, when you awaken, take the time to write down your attitudes and expectations about the coming day. What do you feel? Optimism, fear, anxiety, bitterness, pleasure, or resentment? Don't confuse this response tape that is playing with your internal dialogue. The tape is the background noise to your self-talk. So listen carefully to your underlying responses to the prospect of a new day. How do you expect the day to go? Record your internal response each day in as much detail as possible.

Day One

Day Two

Day Three

Day Four

Day Five

Day Six

Day Seven

COMMAND PERFORMANCE

Assume that you have received a message from your boss (or some other more relevant authority figure—spouse's boss, minister or priest, landlord) stating that he/she wants to meet with you at 4:00 today. Write down how you are responding to this command performance internally, given four different circumstances, as follows:

You know you made a mistake.

You know that bad news of some kind related to your involvement with this person is imminent.

You don't have a clue what the meeting might be about.

You know that you are being evaluated regarding your performance in association with this person.

Now repeat the exercise. This time assume that someone personally related to you—spouse, parent or other relative, friend, child—has asked if they can meet with you later to sit down and talk. Record your internal response, given each of the following four scenarios:

There is a problem in the relationship.

Something bad, tragic, or wrong has recently occurred.

You don't have a clue what the meeting is about.

You have not spoken, or not spoken intimately, with this person in a long time.

ASSESSING YOUR TAPES

As you review the responses you have recorded above, what patterns or similarities do you find? Write down your first impressions of any negative self-talk that you uncovered as you completed the preceding exercises.

What scenarios seem to generate negative self-talk?

Do your tapes have to do with work-related encounters? If so, what are the tapes saying?

Are your tapes about particular family members or acquaintances? If so, who are the people and what do your tapes tell you?

Pick out any element of the preceding exercises that helped you identify a tape—preperformance, anticipating a day, facing a meeting, performing a task. Identify whatever common threads or patterns you find.

SCRIPT ASSESSMENT

The work you've done so far in this section should have helped you slow down your tapes and fixed beliefs sufficiently that you can listen to them. Keep in mind that they create the scripts from which you are living. In order to assess each script that is at work in your life, you need to identify the script and analyze it for positive and negative elements. Use the information you've already collected to help you think this through and write it out below.

NAME THAT SCRIPT

The best way to get a handle on this aspect of your fictional self is to think in terms of the roles you identify with yourself. For each role—friend, parent, child, cheerleader, spouse, invalid, athlete, and so on—you have developed a script for what you should say and do, and for what you should expect from others in response. You will find elements of other internal factors in your script. So take some time to look back over the sections on labels, locus of control, and tapes. All of these will help you identify your scripts in detail. Use the chart below for a number of your scripts. If you need more space, use extra paper and attach it to this section of your book.

Name of Script	List of Activities or Behaviors Called For	Description of How People Responded to You as a Consequence of Enacting This Script
1.	• • • • • • • •	
2.	• •	

Name of Script	List of Activities or Behaviors Called For	Description of How People Responded to You as a Consequence of Enacting This Script
	• • • • • •	
3.	• • • • • • • •	
4.	• • • • • • • •	
5.	• • • • • • •	

Name of Script	List of Activities or Behaviors Called For	Description of How People Responded to You as a Consequence of Enacting This Script
6.	• • • • • • • •	
7.	• • • • • • •	
8.	• • • • • •	
9.	• • • • •	

Name of Script	List of Activities or Behaviors Called For	Description of How People Responded to You as a Consequence of Enacting This Script
	• • •	
10.	• • • • • • • •	

INVESTIGATING THE EVIDENCE

Now that you've identified in detail a number of the scripts that you play in your life, let's unpack them so we understand how they serve or detail an authentic concept of self in your life.

1. First, circle those roles you felt to be most in keeping with what you want your life to be. In other words, if you were describing yourself to another person, what scripts would you be most proud to share and have that person know about you? Another way to put it is: Which roles did you enjoy playing? These are the scripts you should circle.

2. Put checks next to those roles you absolutely hated having to play. If you were describing yourself to another person, these would be the roles you are most ashamed of.

3. For every script you've identified, positive or negative, write two paragraphs about whoever it was in your life that had the biggest role in imposing that particular script. Then write two paragraphs about why you think that person cast you in that role and what they got out of it.

Script #1

Who had the biggest role?

Why did they cast you in that role? What did they get out of it?

Script #2

Who had the biggest role?

Why did they cast you in that role? What did they get out of it?

Script #3

Who had the biggest role?

Why did they cast you in that role? What did they get out of it?

Script #4

Who had the biggest role?

Why did they cast you in that role? What did they get out of it?

Script #5

Who had the biggest role?

Why did they cast you in that role? What did they get out of it?

Script #6

Who had the biggest role?

Why did they cast you in that role? What did they get out of it?

Script #7

Who had the biggest role?

Why did they cast you in that role? What did they get out of it?

Script #8

Who had the biggest role?

Why did they cast you in that role? What did they get out of it?

Script #9

Who had the biggest role?

Why did they cast you in that role? What did they get out of it?

Script #10

Who had the biggest role?

Why did they cast you in that role? What did they get out of it?

PLAYING THE PART

The list of scripts and descriptions you have composed give you precious information for creating a new present and future out of the past which has bound you until now. Your scripts are packed with powerful emotions, both positive and negative. You need to identify which roles create which emotions in your life.

With that in mind, and making sure you have the privacy and the time to do it properly, I want you to play out each of the roles you have identified. Actually project yourself into a time, place, and event in which each role was at work in your life. As you do this, talk it out loud to yourself. Speak your thoughts and actions as though you were really there. Don't be embarrassed. This is for you alone, and I guarantee that if you do as I suggest, you will begin to feel again what each role embodies for you emotionally. After you have acted out each role, name the feelings that came over you in the process. They may be negative. They may be positive. Whatever they are, identify them in writing in the space provided.

Script #1

What feelings did you experience as you acted out this script?

Script #2

What feelings did you experience as you acted out this script?

Script #3

What feelings did you experience as you acted out this script?

Script #4

What feelings did you experience as you acted out this script?

Script #5

What feelings did you experience as you acted out this script?

Script #6

What feelings did you experience as you acted out this script?

Script #7

What feelings did you experience as you acted out this script?

Script #8

What feelings did you experience as you acted out this script?

Script #9

What feelings did you experience as you acted out this script?

Script #10

What feelings did you experience as you acted out this script?

YOUR DREAM SCRIPT

As you are working through your scripts, it's important to remember that this isn't an empty set of exercises meant to stir up your past and your feelings. This is all adding up to reconnecting with your authentic self and living in accordance with who you really are and what you really want. By now, you should be exploring in earnest the story you want to write for your own life and the role you want to play in it. You have an opportunity right now to write a script that is truly yours and no one else's. Right this minute, write in as much detail as possible the life script that you would write for yourself if all choices were open to you. Let yourself dream. What would you do if you could do anything? What emotion would you feel and with whom would you share it? Have fun. Explore. Take this opportunity to know yourself and your deepest dreams.

11 PUTTING THE PLAN TO WORK

Before you begin this portion of The Self Matters Companion, *read the Introduction to the Five-Step Action Plan Section and chapter 11 (pages 250–286) of* Self Matters: Creating Your Life from the Inside Out.

If you have completed all the exercises in all the sections leading up to this one, you should congratulate yourself. You have done a powerful piece of preparation for making the rest of your life much more attuned to who you really are and what you really want. I hope that, already, you've gained clarity and insight about your personal history. And I hope that it has eased the burdens you have been carrying as a result of a distorted self-concept.

Now it's time to put all this preparation to the most important work you can do. What you've done so far gives you all the information you need to begin to redefine your life and your self-concept. The exercises that follow provide the tools that allow you not only to understand and analyze where you are and how you got there, but also to choose a different future.

I've been your guide in this journey. But the real power to change resides within you alone. You must take responsibility for your life as it is. And you must be accountable and action-oriented in regard to what you do about it. As you work through each of the five steps in the Action Plan, you will be reliving the defining moments, revisiting the critical choices, and facing the pivotal people of your life. You may feel long-term pain in a fresh way. But you will also experience the power that comes from rejecting the false messages you have accepted about yourself and your ability to be, think, and do differently.

The coming pages guide you through one cycle of the Five-Step Action Plan. Before you complete this, you will need to review all that you wrote in the sections of this companion that covered external factors—defining moments, critical choices, and pivotal people. What I want you to do is select from among those exercises one moment, choice, or person on which you will concentrate as your target life factor. I'll explain what you're looking for in Step 1. From there, you'll work through all the five steps with that one factor as your focus.

After the first cycle, you'll find a second set of pages that provide you a guide in which to repeat the five steps with another target factor. I suggest that you use the second set of pages as a master set for photocopying multiple sets. These can provide you with guided journal space to complete the five steps with as many target factors from your life as you choose to tackle. The more attention and focus you give this, the more you will make the tools for healing and redefinition your own. Any event or factor in your life that is important to you and your self-concept is important enough to be given your full attention and effort.

Let's begin.

STEP 1: TARGET THE EVENT

Set aside at least an hour and reserve a quiet, private place for yourself. Make sure you are comfortable enough that issues of physical comfort don't distract you (but not so comfortable that you're tempted to take a nap!). You may or may not be able to complete these steps in a single sitting. That's okay. It's only important that you commit yourself to seeing the entire five steps through and then honor that commitment.

Looking back at what you recorded in the External Factors section of *Self Matters*, decide which, among those key external factors you identified (moments, choices, or people), has been the *single most toxic factor in your life.* That is to say, that this one factor did the greatest amount of damage or left the most destructive mark on your concept of yourself.

Write a short description of that target event. You need write only a few sentences. What you write may be almost identical to what you wrote about the event earlier. Or, changes in your perceptions or perspective since that writing may mean that you want to describe the event in different terms now.

Look at what you have just written. Do you still believe that this is the most toxic moment? Have you been completely truthful in your description? Getting the mess out there in honest terms is an important step in being able to clean up the mess. And cleaning up the mess is what we want to do.

STEP 2: AUDIT YOUR INTERNAL RESPONSE TO THAT EVENT
Now that you have an honest, working description of your target event, you will bring the five internal factors to bear on it. These are your locus of control, internal dialogue, labels, tapes, and fixed beliefs. Go back and read what you wrote in those sections of this companion. The work you have already done will help you substantially as you think through your target event. Take warning, though. What you think intellectually that you "ought" to say in response to the following questions may be quite different from what you honestly believe. Tell the truth. *You cannot change what you do not acknowledge.* This is your chance to acknowledge truthfully what you believe so you can change and heal. With your target event in mind, answer each of the following questions:

1. Locus of Control
Where do you place responsibility or blame for the event?

Who decided how you were going to respond to this event?

Were you in control of the situation? Explain.

2. Internal Dialogue

What has been the tone and content of your internal dialogue since that event?

Do you find your real-time, "normal speed" conversations in your daily life reflecting the changes that occurred within you associated with that event?

When you reflect on the event, what do you say to yourself?

When you're not reflecting directly on the event, but it causes you to experience negative self-judgments in relation to other events or circumstances, what do you say to yourself?

What was your perception of your behavior and the behavior of others involved in the event at the time it occurred?

What are you telling yourself about those things today?

How does the way in which you perceived yourself and reacted to this event affect your confidence and style of engaging the world?

3. Labels
What labels have you generated for yourself as a result of your event? That is, what have you told yourself about you?

4. Tapes
What tapes has this event generated or contributed to? Explore the expected outcomes or predictions that linger in your mind as a result of your external event.

If you suspect that your most stressful situations activate a tape that screams negative messages, what are those messages?

Is the tape a consequence of the event that you're addressing here? If so, explain how.

5. Fixed Beliefs

What are the fixed beliefs and resulting life script that you have constructed as a result of this event?

How have you limited yourself as a result of this event?

Look for and describe the specific connections between your fixed beliefs and this event.

STEP 3: TEST YOUR INTERNAL RESPONSES FOR AUTHENTICITY

At this point, you need to equip yourself with some clear-cut criteria for authenticity. You need to develop the standard by which you test your internal responses for whether they ring true to the real you. Each of the four criteria, phrased as questions, I am offering here should be applied to the internal responses you have identified in relation to your target event. As you work through the criteria for authenticity, you should go back and reread what you've written in response to your target event. Apply the questions as honestly as you possibly can. Your answers will allow you to see clearly how authentic or fictional your internal responses are.

1. Is it a true fact?

Is what you are thinking, feeling, perceiving, or assigning something that is objectively, verifiably true? Or is it something you believe now because you believed it when the target event first occurred? Relate this question to:

Locus of control

Internal dialogue

Labels

Tapes

Fixed beliefs

2. Does holding on to the thought or attitudes serve your best interests?

Does it make you happy, calm, peaceful, and fulfilled? Relate this question to:

Locus of control

Internal dialogue

Labels

Tapes

Fixed beliefs

3. Are your thoughts and attitudes advancing and protecting your health?

You cannot answer yes to this question if your thoughts about yourself push you into high-risk behavior, or if the pain and stress of your responses take a physical toll that you can ill afford. Relate this quetion to:

Locus of control

Internal dialogue

Labels

Tapes

Fixed beliefs

4. Does this attitude or belief get you more of what you want, need, and deserve?

To answer this question, you need first to ask: "What is my goal?" Do your responses to the target event help you reach your goal? Relate this question to:

Locus of control

Internal dialogue

Labels

Tapes

Fixed beliefs

The bottom line here is simple. Every internal response that you become aware of needs to be held up to these four criteria:

Is it a true fact?
Does holding on to the thought or attitude serve your best interest?
Are your thoughts and attitudes advancing and protecting your health?
Do your thoughts and beliefs get you what you want?

When you can answer yes to all four, you know the belief or attitude is passing the test for authenticity. If it doesn't pass, GET RID OF IT. It's a lie and it's hurting you.

STEP 4: COME UP WITH AN AUTHENTICALLY ACCURATE ALTERNATIVE (AAA) RESPONSE

Any internal response that does not pass the test for authenticity is a fictional response. But it is never enough to simply dump the response that does not serve your authentic self. You must fill the void you create with an Authentically Accurate Alternative. In other words, after you figure out what is false, you need to discover and choose what is true. Use the chart that follows to brainstorm alternatives to the fictional beliefs you uncovered using the Authenticity Criteria above. Again, you may want more space than is provided. If so, photocopy the chart or create your own on a separate piece of paper so you can be as complete as possible.

In the left-hand column, list your fictional beliefs related to your target event. In the right-hand column, list as many alternative beliefs as you can.

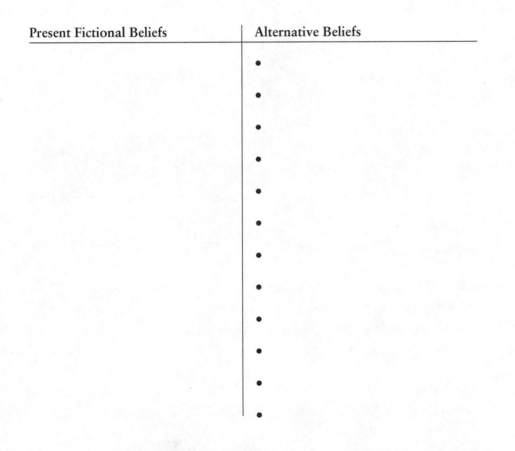

Present Fictional Beliefs	Alternative Beliefs
	•
	•
	•
	•
	•
	•
	•
	•
	•
	•
	•
	•

Present Fictional Beliefs	Alternative Beliefs
	•
	•
	•
	•
	•
	•
	•
	•
	•
	•
	•
	•
	•
	•

Now go back and test each of your alternative beliefs with the Authenticity Criteria:

Is it a true fact?
Does holding on to the thought or attitude serve your best interest?
Are your thoughts and attitudes advancing and protecting your health?
Do your thoughts and beliefs get you what you want?

Put a line through any alternative beliefs that do not pass the test. If you have to cross out all of the alternatives to any particular fictional

belief, go back to the drawing board and brainstorm for alternative beliefs again. Circle any alternatives that pass the test. You are beginning
to find the beliefs that will allow you to live in harmony with your authentic self.

STEP 5: IDENTIFY AND EXECUTE YOUR MINIMAL
EFFECTIVE RESPONSE (MER)

The goal of this final step is emotional closure. You need to be able to
say a last "farewell" to the target event that has had a toxic effect on
your life. Because you are uncovering the damage that has hurt your
authentic concept of self, and you are taking steps to replace the fictional beliefs with authentic ones, you can now let this event go. But
first, you have to *feel* the resolution of your pain. And that will take an
active response on your part.

Understand this: You will not lessen your pain by dumping the max-
imum amount of pain on another person. That has a nasty way of dou-
bling back on you. You will heal your pain by gaining a greater ability
to express the pain you feel in authentic terms, believing that your feelings of hurt or outrage or injustice are valid, and liberating yourself
from the emotional prison they create. In short, the concept of Minimal
Effective Response (MER) seeks to satisfy your need for resolution,
without creating a whole new set of problems.

Minimal Effective Response

Consider the event that you have been analyzing. Let's explore what
your MER might be. Use the four-part test that follows.

1. What action can you take to resolve this pain?

2. If you were successful and achieved this action, how would you feel?

3. Does the feeling you will have match the feeling you *want* to have?

4. Remember the word "minimal": Could there be some other, more emotionally or behaviorally economical action that would give you the emotional resolve you want to feel? If so, what would it be?

Continue this process until you arrive at an acceptable, effective MER. When you have done so, commit yourself to action. Put it in writing here:

I commit myself to (describe the action you have decided on)

I will do this by (give yourself a real-time deadline)

FORGIVENESS THAT SETS YOU FREE

Remember always that when you refuse to forgive the wrong that has been done you, you chain yourself to the negative emotions that have distorted your concept of self. In other words, you perpetuate the negative impact of the events that have shaped you. You don't forgive another person only if or when they deserve it. People often *don't* deserve forgiveness. You forgive because, by doing so, you release yourself from the bitterness and hatred and anger that bind you. Consider the external factor you have targeted. Write out what you would feel—and the changes in your life that could occur—if you could genuinely lay it down and move beyond it.

STARTING TODAY

Write a paragraph that describes the most surprising insight you have gained as you applied the Five-Step Action Plan to your target event. What have you discovered about yourself? About the pain you have carried? About forgiveness?

FIVE-STEP ACTION PLAN

Use this shortened form, referring to the one you've already used when necessary, to continue to work through other external factors you have identified as important to your self-concept. Make copies of the form *before* you start writing, and use the copies rather than this master, so you can make additional copies as you need them.

STEP 1: TARGET THE EVENT

Looking back at what you recorded in the External Factors section of the *Self Matters Companion,* choose one of those key external factors you identified (moments, choices, or people) that has had a distorting or damaging effect on your concept of self.

Write a short description of that target event.

Look at what you have just written. Do you still believe that this is a toxic moment? Have you been completely truthful in your description?

STEP 2: AUDIT YOUR INTERNAL RESPONSE TO THAT EVENT

With your target event in mind, answer each of the following questions:

1. Locus of Control

Where do you place responsibility or blame for the event?

Who decided how you were going to respond to this event?

Were you in control of the situation? Explain.

2. Internal Dialogue

What has been the tone and content of your internal dialogue since that event?

Do you find your real-time, "normal speed" conversations in your daily life reflecting the changes that occurred within you associated with that event?

When you reflect on the event, what do you say to yourself?

When you're not reflecting directly on the event, but it causes you to experience negative self-judgments in relation to other events or circumstances, what do you say to yourself?

What was your perception of your behavior and the behavior of others involved in the event at the time it occurred?

What are you telling yourself about those things today?

How does the way in which you perceived yourself and reacted to this event affect your confidence and style of engaging the world?

3. Labels
What labels have you generated for yourself as a result of your event? That is, what have you told yourself about you?

4. Tapes
What tapes has this event generated or contributed to? Explore the expected outcomes or predictions that linger in your mind as a result of your external event.

If you suspect that your most stressful situations activate a tape that screams negative messages, what are those messages?

Is the tape a consequence of the event that you're addressing here? If so, explain how.

5. Fixed Beliefs

What are the fixed beliefs and resulting life script that you have constructed as a result of this event?

How have you limited yourself as a result of this event?

Look for and describe the specific connections between your fixed beliefs and this event.

STEP 3: TEST YOUR INTERNAL RESPONSES FOR AUTHENTICITY

Apply the questions below as honestly as you possibly can to the internal responses to the target event you have identified. Your answers will allow you to see clearly how authentic or fictional your internal responses are.

1. Is it a true fact?

Is what you are thinking, feeling, perceiving, or assigning something that is objectively, verifiably true? Or is it something you believe now because you believed it when the target event first occurred? Relate this question to:

Locus of control

Internal dialogue

Labels

Tapes

Fixed beliefs

2. Does holding on to the thought or attitude serve your best interests?

Does it make you happy, calm, peaceful, and fulfilled? Relate this question to:

Locus of control

Internal dialogue

Labels

Tapes

Fixed beliefs

3. Are your thoughts and attitudes advancing and protecting your health?

You cannot answer yes to this question if your thoughts about yourself push you into high-risk behavior, or if the pain and stress of your responses take a physical toll that you can ill afford. Relate this question to:

Locus of control

Internal dialogue

Labels

Tapes

Fixed beliefs

4. Does this attitude or belief get you more of what you want, need, and deserve?
To answer this question, you need first to ask: "What is my goal?" Do your responses to the target event help you reach your goal? Relate this question to:

Locus of control

Internal dialogue

Labels

Tapes

Fixed beliefs

STEP 4: Come Up with an Authentically Accurate Alternative (AAA) Response
In the left-hand column, list your fictional beliefs related to your target event. In the right-hand column, list as many alternative beliefs as you can.

Present Fictional Beliefs	Alternative Beliefs
	•
	•
	•
	•
	•
	•
	•
	•
	•
	•
	•
	•
	•

Present Fictional Beliefs	Alternative Beliefs
	•
	•
	•
	•
	•
	•
	•
	•
	•
	•
	•
	•

Now go back and test each of your alternative beliefs with the Authenticity Criteria.

Is it a true fact?

Does holding on to the thought or attitude serve your best interest?

Are your thoughts and attitudes advancing and protecting your health?

Do your thoughts and beliefs get you what you want?

Put a line through any alternative beliefs that do not pass the test. If you have to cross out all of the alternatives to any particular fictional belief, go back to the drawing board and try again. Circle any alternatives that pass the test. You are beginning to find the beliefs that will allow you to live in harmony with your authentic self.

STEP 5: IDENTIFY AND EXECUTE YOUR MINIMAL EFFECTIVE RESPONSE (MER)

The goal of this final step is emotional closure. Use the concept of Minimal Effective Response (MER) to find some way to satisfy your need for resolution, without creating a whole new set of problems.

Minimal Effective Response
Consider the event that you have been analyzing. Let's explore what your MER might be. Use the four-part test that follows.

1. What action can you take to resolve this pain?

2. If you were successful and achieved this action, how would you feel?

3. Does the feeling you will have match the feeling you *want* to have?

4. Remember the word "minimal": Could there be some other, more emotionally or behaviorally economical action that would give you the emotional resolve you want to feel? If so, what would it be?

Continue this process until you arrive at an acceptable, effective MER. When you have done so, commit yourself to action. Put it in writing here:

I commit myself to (describe the action you have decided on)

I will do this by (give yourself a real-time deadline)

FORGIVENESS THAT SETS YOU FREE

Consider the external factor you have targeted. Write out what you would feel if you could genuinely lay it down and move beyond it.

12 SABOTAGE

Before you begin this portion of The Self Matters Companion, *read chapter 12 (pages 287–303) of* Self Matters: Creating Your Life from the Inside Out.

You've come a long way since you started this book. I hope you feel the excitement for yourself that I feel for you. The knowledge and tools that you have gained through the exercises and challenges of *Self Matters* have put you well on the road toward reconnecting with your authentic self and life.

But I don't want you to go forward like a lamb to the slaughter. It's important for you to acknowledge and understand what you have probably often intuited—that friends and family may present the biggest challenges yet to the changes you want and need to make. Their support and empathy may be the last thing you can count on, because your changes look scary and feel threatening from the outside. The people around you are not in control, and that troubles them. They cannot predict what comes next, and that frightens them. And they may not have the courage to do likewise, which makes them feel bad about themselves. It all adds up to them holding you to the way you've always been and, to their way of thinking, always ought to be.

Understanding this is important, but it isn't enough. You need to have a clear sense of the forms of sabotage that you will probably face. You need to get a feel for when and how the sabotage is likely to appear. And, most of all, you need to create a plan of action for yourself in response to sabotage. If you wait until it is happening, I can guarantee that you'll be tempted to cave in to the pressure. If you go into your relationships and situations with the expectation of sabotage and a plan of action ready, you'll stand in a far stronger position to keep moving forward in your own process of growth and positive change.

The bottom line is simple: The rest of the world is not devoted to nurturing you. What it wants is compliance and conformity, whether or not that allows you to build a life that is vibrant, passionate, and full of living color. It is up to you to reconnect with the gifts, talents, desires, and dreams that form the core of your authentic self. The rest of the world will come along or it won't. Unless you've decided to betray yourself for the sake of the comfort of others, you'll just have to let the world go. You may be surprised at how people can come back around when you stand up for your real self.

The following exercises will help you zero in on the specific people and particular categories of sabotage that you have experienced. Handle them gently but honestly. They are not intended to give you a list of "bad guys." They are meant to help you identify negative dynamics that keep you from your forward motion. You can throw out the obstructive behaviors and responses without rejecting the people. Let your heart and your head be a team as you work through this.

YOU'RE RAINING ON MY PARADE . . .

Think back to times in your life when you have tried to make a personal change for the better. It may have related to your physical appearance or well-being. It may have concerned education. It may have had to do with your spiritual life. Or it may have included seeking professional help for psychological distress. In one way or another, you were seeking to take a positive step for yourself. If your experience is like the experience of every other human being, you found out that other people don't like it when you change or try to change.

Review the different periods of your adult life. When have you attempted to make a positive change for yourself? What was the change? What did you do about it? Look at the list below. Put a checkmark to the left of every statement that describes some time in your life. If you can change any statement to make it more applicable to you, do so.

Just write in your own changes. If you remember a situation that does not appear on the list, add it.

_____ I tried to lose excess weight.

_____ I tried to shape up with a new exercise program and/or a membership at a gym.

_____ I tried to further my education.

_____ I tried to get a better job.

_____ I tried to get professional help for my marriage/significant relationship.

_____ I tried to focus on better nutrition.

_____ I tried to learn how to do things on time.

_____ I tried to do a better job of keeping my home/office/desk organized and neat.

_____ I tried to cut out the rich desserts.

_____ I tried to spend more time in personal meditation and/or prayer.

———— I tried to make regular special time for my spouse/significant other.

———— I tried to put a stop to my impulse shopping.

———— I tried to forgive someone for an old wound and end a grudge.

———— I tried not to participate in the neighborhood gossip.

Now, put yourself back in that time and place and let your memory work for you. Did you encounter resistance to your efforts to change? If so, in the space below each of the items you checked off above, describe who made it difficult for you to do what you set out to do. What did this person say or do that made your commitment hard to keep? Write it down.

SABOTAGE ASSESSMENT

What we're talking about is the dynamic of sabotage. You probably identified some situations above in which you felt sabotaged by a family member, friend, or colleague. Now let's review why such a thing happens. Read the descriptions listed here for each of the categories of sabotage.

(O) =   **Overprotection:** essentially, a message of fear that you will fail.

(P) =   **Power manipulation:** a negative response motivated by the other's fear of losing power over you or of you becoming self-empowered.

(L) =   **Leveling:** in general, a response based on jealousy that causes the other to work *for* you when you're failing and *against* you when you're succeeding.

(S) =   **Safety in the status quo:** resistance to change based on fear of change, even if change would be for the better.

You may receive any of these responses from someone who cares deeply for you just as readily as from someone who doesn't. Either because of their own misguided understanding of your needs and potential or the threat they feel because of changes you are making, they come back at you with attitudes and actions that undermine your authenticity. They may not realize what they are doing. The important thing is that *you* realize it and take appropriate action in response.

I've described several situations below that many people experience. If any of them apply to your life in some form, score how another person or persons try to sabotage your efforts to change by circling O, P, L, or S. This should also help you to better understand how these different categories of sabotage work.

1. When you were trying to lose weight and go on a diet, your friend/s (family member/s, colleague/s, etc.) seemed to understand and support at first, but . . .

(O) They began to express worry about how much you were depriving yourself of food and told you that they thought you looked bad.

(P) They began to seem defensive, saying that they thought that you were trying to be better than they were or that you might be looking for "thinner" friends.

(L) They seemed to become depressed, or even hostile, when you showed success, and even called your weight-loss program a fake or a racket.

(S) They seemed to want you back the way you were, and may even have said that they would be uncomfortable if you were different.

2. When you wanted to stop smoking, your friend/s (family member/s, colleague/s, etc.) agreed with your conclusion that it was unhealthy for you, but . . .

(O) They began to worry that you were becoming more stressed when you wanted to smoke, and they thought that stopping was making you worse.

(P) They began to seem defensive, saying that they thought that you were trying to be better than they were or you might look for "healthier" friends.

(L)   They seemed to become depressed, or even hostile, when you showed success, and seemed to intentionally light up in front of you.

(S)   They seemed to want you back the way you were, and may have said that they would be uncomfortable if you did not smoke.

3. When you had successfully fallen in love with a great person and your relationship with this person was definitely better than anything you had experienced before (and appeared different from your friends' [or family member's/s' or colleague's/s', etc.] relationships), they seemed supportive at first, but . . .

(O)   They began to worry that you were not being cautious enough and warned that you might get hurt; because you really did not know the person yet.

(P)   They seemed to be resistant to your relationship, expressing suspicion about the other person.

(L)   They seemed to be depressed and isolated you at times because you did not have the same relationship problems they did.

(S)   They seemed to want you to have the same problems you had always had or that they had, and seemed focused on the problems.

4. When you had decided to change your career and might have needed to go back to school, your friend/s (family member/s, colleague/s, etc.) may have applauded your ambition at first, but . . .

(O)   They seemed to worry that you would fail and be disappointed in yourself.

(P)   They seemed worried that you would eventually look down on them if you were successful.

(L)   They seemed to become depressed and expressed the fear that you would not have anything in common with them and would no longer be their friend.

(S)   They began to put down your intended goal or new aspirations by declaring that people who had attained what you were trying for had turned out to be unhappy.

5. When you were diagnosed with a medical problem that demanded a change in your lifestyle (such as drinking less alcohol, weighing less, being less stressed, exercising more, etc.), your friends (family member/s, colleague/s, etc.) may have supported this important change, but . . .

(O) They began to worry about how much you were depriving yourself of things you used to enjoy and expressed that they thought you were looking bad.

(P) They began to seem defensive, saying that they thought you were trying too hard: "After all, you have the genes for your medical problem. All you can really do is take the medicine . . ."

(L) They seemed to become depressed, even hostile, when you showed success, and may even have called your program quackery or a racket.

(S) They seemed to want you back the way you were, even if it contributed to you getting sick, and they may have said that they would be uncomfortable if you changed.

6. If you decided to buy a new house, bigger or better than your friend/s (family member/s, colleague/s, etc.), they . . .

(O) Expressed worry that you might not be able to make the payments and would create problems for yourself.

(P) Expressed the notion that you were moving into a "classier neighborhood" and would probably never come back.

(L) Seemed depressed and ready to dismiss you quickly, as if you no longer belonged to the group.

(S) Told stories of people they knew who had moved away and were very unhappy.

7. If you or your mate had received a substantial raise in salary or a promotion to a higher position, your friend/s (family member/s, colleague/s, etc.) . . .

(O)   Expressed concern that you probably would not be able to do all the things necessary for your new position (like working late, traveling, etc.), and so you might want to reconsider.

(P)   Seemed defensive and began to treat you as an outsider, even like a part of the "upper crust," leaving you out of normal conversations.

(L)   Seemed to condemn you for taking the job, as though it were an affront to them.

(S)   Seemed to be afraid of what you might tell others about them, as if you would snitch on them.

8. If you strongly considered changing your relationship (as in filing for a divorce), even after a long time of abuse, your friend/s (family member/s, colleague/s, etc.) likely supported your determination and frustration; but if/when you followed through with it, they . . .

(O)   Warned you of the problems in being alone and fending for yourself.

(P)   Gave you the feeling that you were doing something morally wrong, even though you had discussed the relationship's problems on many, many occasions before with no such response.

(L)   Offered support for your problems, but made clear their lack of support for action.

(S)   Discussed what your station in life should be, and your need to learn to accept it.

9. If you learned that you had some latent form of diabetes and would have to limit your sugar intake, but one of your ongoing rituals with your friend/s (family member/s, colleague/s, etc.) was to have cheesecake and ice cream, they . . .

(O)   Offered alternatives so that you could continue to eat sugar with them, such as going totally sugar-free the rest of the time or drinking a lot of water or tea after the ritual with them.

(P)   Condemned your medical practitioners as quacks and stupid, since you were just fine, and: "They have medicine that would take care of eating sugar anyway."

(L)   Became angry with you because you were diagnosed with this problem.

(S)   Continued to think of you as you always have been and offered you the sugar dessert, even if you did not eat it.

10. If you won or had been given a trip to an exotic place, your friend/s (family member/s, colleague/s) . . .

(O)   Changed the subject after a short celebration comment, and talked about you after you left.
(P)   Became angry or hostile.
(L)   Said something in the spirit of: "Don't think you are too special."
(S)   Minimized your award and discussed unrelated, mundane things.

Do you see any pattern in the way that you are most often sabotaged? If so, what is it?

As you remember and assess ways in which you have been sabotaged, can you identify any category of sabotage that you find particularly difficult to withstand? If so, what is it?

PREPARING FOR SABOTAGE

You don't have to make yourself a sitting duck for sabotage. Neither do you have to label others who resist your changes as "the enemy." What you should do is focus on how other people might sabotage your efforts to reconnect with your authentic self, no matter how noble or loving their reasons. The following exercises can help you recognize and prepare for the most likely sources and categories of sabotage in your life.

STEP 1
Give yourself some time for this one. You need to look back over the situations described above with which you identified and put some

faces to what happened. There may be other situations that have come to mind for you, as well. Again, you need to get personal, but ideally without casting blame. In the left-hand column of the chart that follows, write down the names of the people who might sabotage you in your quest for your authentic life. In the center column, write down the category or probable method of their likely sabotage (overprotection, power manipulation, leveling, or safety in the status quo).

Possible Saboteur	Probable Method of Sabotage	My Response

STEP 2

You know the people you've listed—who they are, what they mean to you, and probably what they intend when they try to sabotage your efforts to reconnect to your authentic self. Given your personal knowledge of each of these people, how will you respond to their sabotage? Smile, be grateful, but courteously deflect their interference? Or directly assert your rejection of the sabotage they are dealing you?

Think about what will most likely promote your authentic life. Think, too, about how you will feel after you respond in the way that you plan to do. Write out your response to each saboteur in the far right-hand column. Don't be afraid to tell it like it is if that's what's needed. None of the people you've listed is ultimately going to give you what you need to be authentic. Only you can do that. The quality of their friendship and connection will be proved in what they make of all the great changes yet ahead of you.

SEE YOU IN THE SUNLIGHT!

You've done a considerable amount of work in this book. And it's a great start to the rest of your life. You've built up some potent, positive momentum. Now it's time for you to make the next important steps. Start taking action right this minute. You may have more you want to do with specific exercises in this book. You may have relationships or work options or physical improvements that you are ready to focus on in relation to your blossoming authentic self. Whatever the "next" step is for you, start now. Write out what it is you need to work on. Describe what you need to do. Be specific, with a timetable and a strategy included. Whatever you're about to embark on, describe it in specific, attainable, measurable terms.

Commit yourself to revisiting what you've written here in a month. Ask yourself: "Am I doing what I pledged to do? If not, what do I need to do to make it happen? If so, what do I need to do next?" Above all, take the time to love your life and what it is becoming. Now is your moment to stand up for your authenticity. Go for it!

My date with myself for review is